Spirit Search

Spirit Search

Discovering What the Bible Teaches About the Holy Spirit

B.G. Hamon

Pathway
PRESS

ALL SCRIPTURE QUOTATIONS, unless otherwise indicated, are from the King James Version of the Bible.

Scripture quotations marked *NKJV* are from the *New King James Version*. Copyright © 1979, 1980, 1982, 1990, 1995, Thomas Nelson Inc., Publishers.

Scripture quotations marked *NIV* are taken from the Holy Bible, *New International Version*®. *NIV*®. Copyright © 1973, 1978, 1984 by International Bible Society. Used by permission of Zondervan Publishing House. All rights reserved.

Library of Congress Catalog Card Number: 2001093501
ISBN: 0-87148-636-9
Copyright ©2001 by Pathway Press
Cleveland, Tennessee 37320
All Rights Reserved
Printed in the United States of America

Dedication

It is with love and pride that I dedicate this book to

Dot (Dorothy Aycock Hamon)

my wife of 51 years.

She gave her heart to Jesus at age five
and was baptized in the Holy Spirit at age 13.

She gave herself to me at age 18, and has been the
anchor of my ministry and my life ever since.

She is a model mother for our five children,
an exemplary preacher's wife and an
effective teacher at school, home and church.

She exemplifies Solomon's role model for Proverbs 31.

Contents

Introduction 9

1. What Is Baptism in the Holy Spirit? . . 13
2. Is Spirit Baptism the Same
   as Being Saved? 23
3. The Initial Evidence of
   Holy Spirit Baptism 35
4. Are Tongues the Only Evidence
   of the Spirit Baptism? 45
5. The Gifts of the Holy Spirit 59
6. Was Speaking in Tongues
   for Apostles Only? 69
7. Some Objections and Spiritual Abuses . . 87
8. How To Receive the Baptism
   in the Holy Spirit 95

To the Pastor 109
An Appeal to the Honest Seeker 111

Bibliography 113

Introduction

When Joel foretold the promise of the baptism in the Holy Spirit 600 years before the initial occurrence on the Day of Pentecost (see Joel 2:28, 29; Acts 2:1-4), he could have added the footnote, "and it will create a continuous debate and controversy in the church world for centuries." No other doctrine or subject is so widely discussed, debated, opposed or proclaimed as the Holy Spirit baptism and its subsequent results and effects.

The Christian church is and was divided into different camps of support and opposition to both the doctrine and the experience of the baptism in the Holy Spirit. The more the doctrine has been accepted, the more the experience has been received.

Opposition has increased as a result. Conservative estimates by reliable sources say that the number of Christians who have received the baptism in the Holy Spirit with the evidence of speaking in tongues now exceeds 400 million worldwide. In most countries, members of traditionally non-Pentecostal churches have received this experience. They are enjoying the spiritual benefit and the experience, even when they do not fully understand its scriptural implications.

The popularity and acceptance of the experience has given rise to many new movements and groups. While we rejoice over this fact, we must also admit that it has had some regrettable negative results. In some circles the newfound ecstasy and joy of this phenomenon has resulted in unscriptural practices and teachings.

Unfortunately, spiritual excess and abuse of the gifts of the Spirit have done injustice to the genuine power received when one is baptized in the Holy Spirit.

False teachings arise when unharnessed zeal exceeds a solid Bible teaching on any subject. Sincere and well-meaning people can be led astray unless they are grounded in the Word of God and are willing to be taught by Scripture—or at least by seasoned and experienced leaders who have proven their integrity and stood the test of time.

As author of this book, I assume no exceptional position of authority, experience or superiority in any way on this subject. It is not my wish to be argumentative or confrontational. My earnest desire and only purpose is to give sound, rational and scriptural guidance in answer to "What meaneth this?" (Acts 2:12). My prayer is that those who are hungry for more of God's blessings will find instruction in this book that results in many receiving the baptism in the Holy Spirit.

Admittedly, this book is not an exhaustive study of the Holy Spirit. It is, at best, a brief treatment and study of Scripture. It can be a beginning for the honest-hearted seeker to launch a quest for an experience with God that opens a new dimension of spiritual life—"joy unspeakable and full of glory" (1 Peter 1:8).

With the Bible I will answer these and other questions:

1. What is the baptism in the Holy Spirit?

2. Is this a separate experience from salvation?

3. Is speaking in tongues the initial evidence of the Holy Spirit baptism?

4. Is speaking in tongues the only evidence?

5. Is the baptism in the Holy Spirit optional for the Christian?

6. Was the baptism in the Holy Spirit only for the early church?

Examine these pages with an open mind, an honest heart and a searching spirit. Have your Bible handy as you study so you can validate and verify the answers to the above questions.

The Word of God provides an unshakable foundation for your discovery and the experience of knowing that "this promise [gift] is for you" (Acts 2:39, *NIV*).

CHAPTER 1

What Is the Baptism in the Holy Spirit?

The questions we propose to answer in this book begin, of necessity, with, "What is the baptism in the Holy Spirit?" All the other questions we may have hinge on this one.

A Fulfillment of Prophecy

More than 600 years before Pentecost, the prophet Joel foretold of the coming of the Holy Spirit in His fulness in this manner:

> And it shall come to pass afterward, that I will pour out my spirit upon all flesh; and your sons and your daughters shall prophesy, your old men shall dream dreams, your young men shall see visions: And also upon the servants and upon the handmaids in those days will I pour out my spirit (Joel 2:28, 29).

On the Day of Pentecost, the apostle Peter gave a direct and clear answer to the question of the onlookers in the Upper Room: "What meaneth this?" (Acts 2:12). His answer, "This is that which was spoken by the prophet Joel" (v. 16), verifies the occasion as a fulfillment of prophecy.

An earlier prophecy by Isaiah declared, "For with stammering lips and another tongue will he speak to this people" (Isaiah 28:11).

A Fulfillment of Promise

Jesus, on various occasions, promised the coming of the Holy Spirit and told of His work.

- "These signs shall follow them that believe; In my name shall they cast out devils; they shall speak with new tongues [by the Holy Spirit] (Mark 16:17).

- "Even the Spirit of truth [Holy Spirit]; whom the world cannot receive, because it seeth him not, neither knoweth him: but ye know him; for he dwelleth with you, and shall be in you" (John 14:17).

- "But the Comforter, which is the Holy Ghost, whom the Father will send in my name, he shall teach you all things, and bring all things to your remembrance" (John 14:26).

- "When the Comforter [the Holy Spirit] is come . . . he shall testify of me" (John 15:26).

- "When he, the Spirit of truth, [the Holy Spirit] is come . . . he shall not speak of himself; but whatsoever he shall hear, that shall he speak" (John 16:13).

These are a few of the promises Jesus gave His disciples either directly or by inference. He gave one of the most direct promises as He was about to be taken up from them on Mount Olivet: "For John truly baptized with water, but ye shall be baptized with the Holy Ghost not many days hence" (Acts 1:5). In John 20:22, Jesus said, "Receive ye the Holy Ghost."

An Impartation of Power

Undeniably, the Holy Spirit was operative in the world before Pentecost. It is also evident that at Pentecost, and since, the Holy Spirit was and is emphasized; He prominently does His work in the church and individuals. The baptism in the Holy Spirit makes a believer's experience and relationship with God a more personal and individual one. Certainly, the Holy Spirit is both active and operative in the experiences of:

Conviction of sin (Titus 1:9; Jude 1:14, 15)

Regeneration (John 3:5; Romans 12:2; Titus 3:5, 1 Peter 1:23)

Sanctification (Acts 26:18; 1 Corinthians 6:11).

In fact, every act of God that man experiences is effected by the Holy Spirit. Still, one may be convinced of God's existence, be aware of Him and even have an experience with God, yet not be baptized in the Holy Spirit. Cornelius in Acts 10 is a classic example.

An Instrument for Revealing God's Love to the Unsaved (Titus 2:11-13)

Jesus showed the prominence of the Holy Spirit's activity in the new birth, "No man can come to me, except the Father which hath sent me draw him" (John 6:44). Then what is the baptism in the Holy Spirit? Jesus said in Acts 1:8:

> But ye shall receive power, after that the Holy Ghost is come upon you: and ye shall be witnesses unto me both in Jerusalem, and in all Judea, and in Samaria, and unto the uttermost part of the earth.

We understand these words, coupled with other statements of Jesus and Biblical writers, to say that the baptism in the Holy Spirit is a prerequisite for one who entering into the ministry of the gospel of the Lord Jesus. Certainly, the task of ministry is no less formidable today than it was to the 70 whom Jesus sent out in pairs, telling them, "Go your ways: behold, I send you forth as lambs among wolves" (Luke 10:3).

The apostle Peter encountered this situation in Jerusalem only days after Pentecost when he and John were arrested for preaching Jesus and the Resurrection (Acts 4:1-12). They were put in prison, then brought before the high priest and council who demanded, "By what power, or by what name, have ye done this?" (v. 7). Many would have been intimidated and fearful, but Peter,

> filled with the Holy Ghost, said unto them . . . Be it known unto you all, and to all the people of Israel, that by the name of Jesus Christ of Nazareth, whom ye crucified, whom God raised from the dead, even by him doth this man stand here before you whole (vv. 8, 10).

This same apostle who weeks earlier displayed such cowardice at the trial of Jesus by denying Him, is now putting his own life at risk for Jesus. What transformation! The baptism in the Holy Spirit made the difference.

The apostle Paul also encountered demonic opposition early in his ministry. When he arrived in Paphos, he discovered that the Holy Spirit baptism, with all of its implications, benefits and power, was for everyone, including the Gentiles. The experience is as much for us today as it was for those who experienced it in the New Testament!

Note that with all the promises Jesus gave His disciples regarding the baptism in the Holy Spirit, they were not confused when it occurred on the Day of Pentecost. Only onlookers were confounded. Only doubters were amazed and did not believe (see Acts 2:12). Obviously, the 120 who were praying, praising and worshiping in one accord in the Upper Room were neither confused, amazed nor in doubt of what was taking place. They expected something unusual, although they were not sure just what, how or when it would happen.

Undoubtedly, they did not understand everything that was going on in the Upper Room. They knew only that they were being filled with exuberant and exciting praise to God—more that ever before in their lives!

Considering these scenarios, can the baptism in the Holy Spirit be optional? The question is, *Why would any believer desire it to be optional?* Some object, saying, "This is the age of enlightenment and information, not regeneration." They continue to try to explain away the reality of the Holy Spirit baptism, choosing to believe that Pentecost was only for the early church and not for us today.

Church history and daily ministerial efforts are full of evidence that education, training and theology, as important as they are, are not by themselves sufficient to do the work of a gospel minister in the care of souls.

A Blessing We Can't Ignore

All over the world, people of every nation are hungry for more of God. They desire a closer walk in the Spirit and want the deeper dimension of life in Him. Thousands are being baptized in the Holy Spirit; they are experiencing more joy and a greater anointing in their lives than ever before.

As on the Day of Pentecost, there is no single method of receiving the baptism in the Holy Spirit. There is no set formula or pattern of action.

Dr. Charles Conn writes in *The Glossolalia Phenomenon* that the Book of Acts gives numerous and varied expressions of how the Holy Spirit comes into the hearts of believers. Here are some of them:

"Ye shall be *baptized* with the Holy Ghost" (Acts 1:5; 11:16)

"The Holy Ghost is come *upon you*" (1:8)

"They were all *filled* with the Holy Ghost" (2:4; 4:31)

"Ye shall *receive* the gift of the Holy Ghost" (2:38)

"Peter, *filled* with the Holy Ghost" (4:8)

"*Full* of the Holy Ghost and wisdom" (6:3)

"*Full* of faith and the Holy Ghost" (6:5)

"*Full* of the Holy Ghost" (7:55)

"They might *receive* the Holy Ghost" (8:15)

"The Holy Ghost was *given*" (8:18)

"He may *receive* the Holy Ghost" (8:19)

"Be *filled* with the Holy Ghost" (9:17)

"The Holy Ghost *fell* on all them which heard the word" (10:44)

"On the Gentiles also was *poured out* the gift of the Holy Ghost" (10:45).

"Which have *received* the Holy Ghost" (10:47)

"God *gave* them the like gift" (11:17)

"*Full* of the Holy Ghost and of faith" (11:24)

"Paul, *filled* with the Holy Ghost" (13:9)

"The disciples were *filled* with joy, and with the Holy Ghost" (13:52)

"Have ye *received* the Holy Ghost . . . ?" (19:2)

"The Holy Ghost *came on them*" (19:6)

These various expressions refer, obviously, to the same, identical impartation of power. Sometimes they are used in close parallel. In Acts 8:16-18 we find the statements, "he was fallen," "they received the Holy Ghost," and "the Holy Ghost was given." These referred to the same outpouring in Samaria.

In Acts 10:44, 45 and 47, we read how "the Holy Ghost fell," "was poured out," and was "received" by those at Cornelius' house. All three expressions refer to the same event. So the baptism in the Holy Spirit is a gift from God the Father to all believers. Indeed, it is a fulfillment of prophecy and a fulfillment of the promises of Jesus to His followers. The prerequisites for receiving the baptism in the Holy Spirit are discussed in another chapter.

God's Gift to You

Nearly everyone delights in receiving gifts. The degree of our delight is determined by the value of the gift. In using *value*, I am not referring to the cost of the gift necessarily . We can no more place a monetary value on the gift of Holy Spirit baptism than we can place a monetary value on forgiveness of sins, the gift of salvation or eternal life. Since the Holy Spirit is the executive of the Godhead, or Trinity, He works in every area of our lives, both physical and spiritual.

In referring to the baptism in the Holy Spirit, we use the pronoun *it* in reference to the experience, but we always say *He* when referring to the Holy Spirit, because He is coequal and coexistent with God and Jesus (see Matthew 28:19; 1 Corinthians 12:4-6, 11; 2 Corinthians 13:14; Revelations 1:4).

To reflect briefly on why we become so excited and thrilled at receiving the baptism in the Holy Spirit, let us consider a small portion of the scope and impact of this heavenly experience on an individual's life. The Holy Spirit lives in you, thus affecting your lives in the following ways:

- He *indwells* on a daily basis (John 14:7).
- He *teaches* (John 14:26).
- He *comforts* (John 14:26).
- He *testifies* (John 15:26).
- He *guides* into all truth (John 16:13).
- He *empowers* (Acts 1:8).
- He gives *wisdom* (Acts 6:3).
- He brings *joy* (Acts 13:52).
- He *commands* (Acts 16:6, 7).
- He *witnesses* (Galatians 4:6).

- He seals believers in the *security* of Jesus (Ephesians 1:13).
- He *reveals* (2 Peter 1:21).
- He *speaks* (Revelations 2:7).

This is only a partial list of blessings included in the baptism in the Holy Spirit, so why would anyone not desire the gift and all that it includes? How can a true believer refrain from praying continually and earnestly for the baptism in the Holy Spirit? My personal resolve is that whatever it takes, I want all that God has for me.

Wisdom and necessity dictates that we should put aside personal prejudice against the baptism in the Holy Spirit. We must forget the tradition of the Fathers who denied the reality of the baptism in the Holy Spirit. We need to be bold in taking God's Word at its face value so that we also may hear the words of the crucified Christ when He "breathed on them, and saith unto them, Receive ye the Holy Ghost" (John 20:22).

"For the promise [gift] is unto you, and to your children, and to all that are afar off, even as many as the Lord our God shall call" (Acts 2:39). The paramount question is not, *Do I have to be baptized in the Holy Spirit?* but rather, *Can I afford not to be baptized in the Holy Spirit?* Why would anyone not want to receive the experience now?

CHAPTER 2

Is Spirit Baptism the Same as Being Saved?

*T*emptation is strong to answer this question with a simple statement, "No, it is not." But that would be oversimplification, and I believe there are many sincere seekers who have a hungry heart for more of God in their lives. Therefore I am compelled to give a complete and clear answer from the Bible. The Word of God gives absolute answers to all who are sincere and honest. So we appeal to the final and highest court of authority, the Scripture.

The Bible reveals the Holy Spirit as the executive member of the Trinity, not just an influence, a presence or even just a power. He is coequal and coexistent with God and the Son (see Matthew 28:19; 1 Corinthians 12:4-6, 11; 2 Corinthians 13:14; Revelations 1:4). He was present and active in the creation of the world (Genesis 1:2). He was one of the "us" in the creation of man (see Genesis 1:26).

Erroneous teachings abound through the worldwide Christian church. Some church leaders declare that one is baptized in the Holy Spirit in the same act and experience of regeneration, conversion, being forgiven of sins, being born again, being saved, accepting Christ as Savior and other terms that refer to the experience of becoming a Christian.

All of these terms are appropriate and are founded in the scriptures; individual preference determines which you choose to use. But regardless of the term one uses, there is no scriptural foundation for teaching that the baptism in the Holy Spirit is the same as being born again.

In fact, thousands of honest, sincere converts have been deprived of the great blessings of the deeper dimensions in the Christian experience because of this teaching. They have found themselves in the same situation as the 12 brethren at Ephesus who told the apostle Paul, "We have not so much as heard whether there be any Holy Ghost" (Acts 19:2). Their quest for more of God's power in their lives is stymied.

Their hunger and yearning for a more satisfying experience with God goes unfulfilled because they have been misled into believing they received all that was available to them when they repented of their sins and accepted Christ as Savior.

The Bible is unmistakably clear: the salvation experience *must* come first (Acts 2:38). Yet, there is another experience available to Christians. They should continue praying, praising and seeking God until that experience becomes reality to them. Doubtlessly, those who teach that Holy Spirit baptism comes with conversion do so in ignorance, even if they are sincere. The end results are deception and disillusionment.

I have no thought of diminishing or minimizing the work of the Holy Spirit in the experience of the new birth. As Dr. R.H. Gause explains,

> It is vitally important to understand that every Christian possesses the Holy Spirit in regeneration measure (Romans 8:9; 1 Corinthians 6:19). This does not assert that every Christian has been baptized with the Holy Spirit. Indwelling and infilling are two completely different experiences. Without the former, one cannot be a child of God at all; without the latter, one cannot be fully effective in His service.

Dr. Ray H. Hughes adds:

> It is not the contention of Pentecostal Christians that true believers do not have the Spirit, for the Bible expressly sets forth the Spirit as the agency of new birth (John 3:8; Romans 4:4, 8:9, 14; Galatians 4:6; Titus 3:5; 1 John 3:24; 4:13). There is a decided difference in the terms ìborn of the Spiritî and ìbaptized in the Holy Spirit.î There is one Holy Spirit, but there are many diversities of operation.

The Reverend Bennie Triplett contends that "Calvary always precedes Pentecost!"

The Book of Acts records the dramatic account of the first group of people experiencing the baptism in the Holy Spirit. We also have the accounts of four other occasions when people received the same experience. An examination of these five instances will answer the question once and for all times that the Holy Spirit baptism is not the same as the new birth or regeneration, and that it does not occur simultaneously in the same act.

I hasten to add that it can and should happen immediately following the new birth experience. However, if one does not experience the baptism in the Holy Spirit immediately after conversion, he or she should not despair but continue praying and seeking God daily until the experience is received. Jesus said, "Tarry until" (see Luke 24:49).

Holy Spirit Baptism at Pentecost

Consider the people filled with the Holy Spirit on the Day of Pentecost—the 120 believers (Acts 1:15).

1. They were followers of Christ (Luke 24:50, 51).
2. They were worshipers of Jesus (v. 52).
3. They obeyed Jesus (v. 53).

Among their number were the 12 original apostles, with the exception of Judas Iscariot (Acts 1:13). The apostles had been in Jesus' ministry for the past three years. They had preached His Word, healed the sick and cast out demons (Matthew 10:7, 8). Can we possibly view these apostles as unbelievers or unregenerate men who had not been saved? No sane person would consider such for even a moment.

Among those in the Upper Room was Mary, the mother of Jesus (Acts 1:4). Again, can any rational person consider this virtuous, holy woman as unregenerate? Hardly! All of them were obviously a part of the group for whom Jesus prayed in the Garden of Gethsemane:

> For I have given unto them the words which thou gavest me; and they have received them, and have known surely that I came out from thee, and they have believed that thou didst sent me (John 17:8).

Yet, with all their close association with Jesus and the marvelous experiences they had with Him, Jesus told the disciples "that they should not depart from Jerusalem, but wait for the promise of the Father" (Acts 1:4).

Christ had given them what we term the Great Commission: "Go ye therefore, and teach all nations [the gospel]" (Matthew 28:19). But before they undertook such a global task, they would need additional equipment and preparations. Jesus described their need when He said,

> But ye shall receive power, after that the Holy Ghost is come upon you: and ye shall be witnesses unto me . . . unto the uttermost part of the earth (Acts 1:8).

Certainly our Lord knew the spiritual status of the people to whom He spoke those words. He knew they were believers in Him and followers of Him. He knew that they had confessed their sins and had been baptized in water. He knew that they would soon be involved in evangelizing the world. Yet He said "Ye shall receive power, after that the Holy Ghost is come upon you" (v. 8).

Converts of Revival in Samaria

It could not be plainer that the 120 believers who received the baptism in the Holy Spirit on the Day of Pentecost were saved and had been followers of Jesus for various periods of time prior to their Spirit baptism.

Another indisputable proof that the baptism in the Holy Spirit does not occur at regeneration, forgiveness of sins or spiritual conversion is found in Acts 8 where the great revival in Samaria is recorded. Philip, one of the deacons of the Jerusalem church, went to Samaria and preached Christ. The whole city "gave heed unto those things which Philip spake. . . . And there was great joy in that city" (Acts 8:6, 8). What pastor anywhere in the world would not rejoice over the thought of having a revival in his church like the one Philip had in Samaria?

News of revivals of that magnitude travel fast and far. Therefore

> when the apostles which were at Jerusalem heard that Samaria had received the word of God, they

> sent unto them Peter and John: Who, when they were come down, prayed for them, that they might receive the Holy Ghost: (For as yet he was fallen upon none of them: only they were baptized in the name of the Lord Jesus [water baptism]) (Acts 8:14-16).

If this account were the only one in the Bible, it would prove beyond question that the baptism in the Holy Spirit is a separate experience from being saved, regenerated, born again or whichever term you prefer. Look closely at the sequence and time frame of the entire narrative in Acts 8.

First, Philip went from Jerusalem to Samaria to preach the gospel to them (v. 5). In that primitive day, with none of the modern conveniences we have (no advertising, no television or newspaper promotion, no organizing team to precede Philip), it is reasonable to assume that the revival lasted for several days. He preached everywhere in the city until "the people with one accord gave heed unto those things which Philip spake" (v. 6).

Second, the impact of the revival was so widespread that, "there was great joy in that city" (v. 8).

Third, the effect of the revival was so compelling that, "when they believed Philip preaching the things concerning the kingdom of God, and the name of Jesus Christ, they were baptized, both men and women" (v. 12).

Fourth, the news of this Samaritan revival reached Jerusalem. Although the two cities were only a few miles apart, it is not logical to think that the apostles heard of it on the same day. After hearing of the revival results, Peter and John went down to Samaria.

When they arrived in the city, they prayed for the revival converts "that they might receive the Holy Ghost" (v. 15). It should be pointed out that the length of time between their conversion in the revival, and the time it took Peter and John to arrive in the city is neither important nor relevant except that it shows that the salvation experience and the Holy Spirit baptism are in no way the same experience.

These new converts who heard the good news of the gospel (v. 5), who believed the gospel and accepted Jesus as Savior (v. 6), who gave a public testimony of accepting Christ in the same manner as we do today, were baptized in water (v. 12). Yet, they still needed another experience with God. Peter and John prayed for them to receive the Holy Spirit baptism (v. 15). "Then laid they their hands on them, and they received the Holy Ghost" (v. 17). Our discussion could be complete if we ended it here, but the Bible gives more irrefutable proof.

Gentiles at Cornelius's House

The Spirit baptism of Cornelius and all who had gathered at his house to hear the sermon of Peter is recorded in Acts 10. To fully understand this event and to put in proper perspective all that is included in it, read the entire chapter. God answered Cornelius's prayers in a miraculous way

(v. 31) and gave him instructions on how to obtain a needed blessing and a deeper experience in God (verse 4-6).

Notice the spiritual status of Cornelius. "A devout man, and one that feared God with all his house, which gave much alms to the people, and prayed to God alway" (v. 2). What pastor of any church in the world would not be happy to have a church full of members like Cornelius?

God thought so highly of Cornelius that He gave a vision and a message of instruction. Can anyone think that Cornelius was not a believer? God gave him specific instructions to send for Peter who would "tell thee what thou oughtest to do" (v. 6). When Peter and his company came to Cornelius's house, they found that "Cornelius waited for them, and had called together his kinsmen and near friends" (v. 24). After exchanging greetings, Peter began his message (v. 34).

Something marvelous and miraculous happened as Peter preached: "While Peter yet spake these words, the Holy Ghost fell on all them which heard the Word" (v. 44). We do not know the number of those who received the baptism in the Holy Spirit at Cornelius's house, we only know that the Spirit came upon "all them which heard the word." Those who were with Simon Peter, "were astonished . . . because that on the Gentiles also was poured out the gift of the Holy Ghost" (v. 45).

How thrilling that this occasion emphasizes God's policy of equality. He does not discriminate against any—especially those who are honest of heart and hungry for more of God. On the Day of Pentecost, Peter told his audience, "the promise [gift] is unto you, and to your children, and to all that are afar off, even as many as the Lord our God shall call" (2:39).

Whether you are rich or poor, bound or free, small or great, royalty or peasant, educated or illiterate, God has the baptism in the Holy Spirit for *you*. As long as God calls people to repentance and discipleship, and as long as the message of Christ is "follow me," He will continue to tell us, "This gift is for you."

Twelve Believers at Ephesus

For the last conclusive evidence that the salvation experience and the baptism in the Holy Spirit are not one and the same, let us examine the record of some Ephesian Christians who received the baptism in the Holy Spirit. This happened when Paul laid hands on them and prayed for them.

In Acts 19, the apostle Paul went to Ephesus, "and finding certain disciples, he said unto them, Have ye received the Holy Ghost since ye believed? And they said unto him, We have not so much as heard whether there be any Holy Ghost" (vv. 1, 2). How sad! Followers of Jesus, disciples of Jesus had never heard "this gift is for you." Who was their pastor? Why had he failed to tell them?

Unfortunately, this is the pitiful plight of thousands throughout the church world today. Good and honest people have accepted Jesus as their Savior, and they are walking in all the light they have. But someone has failed to declare the "whole counsel of God" (Acts 20:27, *NKJV*) to them.

I shudder with fear when I think of preachers who will one day stand before God to give account for their members who say, "We have not heard of the Holy Ghost." Some may say, "Our denomination doesn't teach that," but that response will not be a sufficient answer on the final day.

Paul asked the disciples, "Unto what then were ye baptized? And they said, Unto John's baptism [water baptism]" (v. 3). They were followers of our Lord, and were doubtlessly part of the local church in Ephesus. Paul reminded them, "John verily baptized with the baptism of repentance, saying unto the people, that they should believe on him which should come after him, that is, on Christ Jesus" (v. 4).

Then, "When Paul laid his hands upon them, the Holy Ghost came on them; and they spake with tongues, and prophesied," (v. 6).

While other instances in the Bible also prove that the new birth and the baptism in the Holy Spirit are separate and different experiences, these four incidents are more than sufficient to prove conclusively, without question, that one does not receive the baptism in the Holy Spirit when he or she is regenerated or born again.

It is possible to receive the Holy Spirit baptism in the same service or immediately after repenting of sin and receiving Christ. In fact, this is the ideal. There is no premium to be placed on "tarrying." Contrary to the teachings of some last days neo-Pentecostals, however, one should not be dismayed or reproached for "tarrying until," as Jesus told His followers to do (Luke 24:49). And they did just that! They tarried from the time of His ascension until the Day of Pentecost—10 days.

It doesn't take God a long time to baptize us in the Holy Spirit, but sometimes it takes us a while to prepare our hearts and minds to receive Him. The time element is not the important part of the matter. What really matters is that we experience the dynamic infilling of the Holy Spirit.

"Ye shall receive the gift of the Holy Ghost" (Acts 2:38).

CHAPTER 3

The Initial Evidence of Holy Spirit Baptism

Having established by Scripture in the previous chapters what the baptism in the Holy Spirit is and when we receive Him, we turn, naturally, to the question, "How can I know I have received the Holy Spirit baptism?"

It is impostant to understand that many evidences accompany the Holy Spirit baptism. All result from the experience but the Bible is unmistakably clear and we can see a constant evidence—one which we describe as the "initial physical evidence"—that a person has, indeed, been baptized in the Holy Spirit.

Earl P. Paulk, Sr., explained the word *initial* to mean "placed at the beginning, or first." The word *evidence* means "an outward sign, an indication" or "that which furnishes proof." So while there are many evidences or results of being baptized in the Holy Spirit, one physical evidence manifests itself immediately upon receiving the experience.

Pattern at Pentecost

That physical evidence is *glossolalia*, or speaking with tongues as the Spirit gives utterance. In the Bible it is simply that which was experienced by the 120 believers at Pentecost. "And they were all filled with the Holy Ghost, and began to speak with other tongues, as the Spirit gave them utterance" (Acts 2:4). This is the scriptural pattern for all believers.

That the Peter regarded speaking with tongues as the evidence of the Holy Spirit baptism is clearly shown in his statement to the onlookers and skeptics who gathered in the Upper Room "when this was noised abroad" (v. 6). Peter began his sermon that day with, "these [people] are not drunken as ye suppose" (v. 15). He went on to connect the experience of Pentecost to Jesus, the Son of God.

> This Jesus hath God raised up, whereof we all are witnesses. Therefore being by the right hand of God exalted, and having received of the Father the promise of the Holy Ghost, he hath shed forth this, [what they were witnessing in the Upper Room at that time] which ye now see and hear (v. 32, 33).

Peter left no doubt in the minds of those gathered to witness this strange phenomenon of Holy Spirit baptism. He said, "Ye now see and hear" (v. 33)—in other words, you are seeing and hearing the initial evidence of what has happened. The spectators were amazed.

Some doubted, some mocked, some accused, but none could deny they heard unlearned worshipers praising and glorifying God in the hearers' own languages (v. 8). Not understanding what was happening, they asked in wonder, "What meaneth this?" (v. 12). They could not deny the evidence of what they saw and heard, however.

The experience in Caesarea at the house of Cornelius (Acts 10) shows conclusively that speaking with other tongues is, indeed, the initial evidence of the baptism in the Holy Spirit. It should be noted that Cornelius and all who were in his house at the time were Gentiles.

Heretofore, the Jews believed that only Jews were to receive God's blessings. So when all those in the house were filled with the Holy Spirit, Peter and the Jews who came with him were astonished "that on the Gentiles also was poured out the gift of the Holy Ghost" (v. 45). Notice how Peter and his group knew that the Gentiles had received the Holy Spirit. Luke said, "For [because] they heard them speak with tongues, and magnify God" (v. 46).

When Peter and those with him returned to Jerusalem, he had to defend his ministry to the Gentiles before the "headquarters" people. "When Peter was come up to Jerusalem, they that were of the circumcision contended with him" (11:2). Peter calmed them by recounting the entire sequence of events which took him to Cornelius' house. He told them what took place there (v. 4), and concluded his explanation with this statement:

> And as I began to speak, the Holy Spirit fell on them, as on us at the beginning [Pentecost]. . . . Forasmuch then as God gave them the like gift as He did unto us, [at Pentecost] who believed on the Lord Jesus Christ; what was I, that I could withstand God? (vv. 15, 17).

The conclusion was glorious because "when they heard these things, they held their peace and glorified God" (v. 18). We still glorify God because He is no respecter of persons. To the rich and poor, to the educated and the illiterate, to the bond and the free in every nation on earth, to all people of all times, God's message is the same that it has always been: "The promise is unto you, and to your children, and to all that are afar off, even as many as the Lord our God shall call" (Acts 2:39).

Both at Pentecost and at Cornelius' house, speaking in tongues was convincing physical evidence that people were baptized in the Holy Spirit. In Ephesus (Acts 19), the 12 brethren who were baptized in the Holy Spirit when Paul laid his hand on them and prayed for them "spake with tongues, and prophesied" (v. 6). These are scriptural examples of speaking in tongues as the initial evidence of the Spirit baptism.

Some argue there is no mention of the Samaritans speaking in tongues when they were baptized in the Holy Spirit (Acts 8). Nor does the Bible say that Paul spoke with tongues when he was baptized in the Holy Spirit (Acts 9). I urge you to look more closely at what I believe is convincing evidence, in both cases, that they did speak with tongues as in the three instances mentioned above.

Support in Samaria

The Samaritan revival came when Philip, a deacon in the church at Jerusalem, was led by the Holy Spirit after Pentecost to go to the city of Samaria and preach Christ. Wonderful results were seen when "the people with one accord gave heed unto those things which Philip spake, hearing and seeing the miracles which he did" (Acts 8:6).

The revival results were so far-reaching that "there was great joy in that city" (v. 8). The Samaritans believed and were baptized in water, but they did not immediately receive the baptism in the Holy Spirit.

I point this out to show that one is not baptized in the Holy Spirit in the act of regeneration, or being saved. After the Samaritans believed for salvation, it remained for them to be filled with the Holy Spirit. And they were—very soon.

> Now when the apostles which were at Jerusalem heard that Samaria had received the word of God, they sent unto them Peter and John: Who, when they were come down, prayed for them, that they might receive the Holy Ghost: (For as yet he was fallen upon none of them: only they were baptized in the name of the Lord Jesus.) Then laid they [the apostles] their hands on them [the new converts], and they received the Holy Ghost (vv. 14-17).

Three points in this narrative should be carefully noted:

1. They first had to believe for salvation.

2. They were baptized in water as a testimony to their conversion, even though that sequence is not a prerequisite. At Cornelius's house in Caesarea, believers were baptized with the Holy Spirit first, and then were taken out for water baptism.

3. The writer of Acts does not specify that they spoke with tongues when filled with the Holy Spirit, but an unprejudiced reading of the account strongly suggests they did. Without question, the Holy Spirit's coming upon them was evidenced by observable signs. Those signs captured the attention of the sorcerer who offered the apostles money to give him the power to do as they had done to the Samaritans (v. 18).

In keeping with the context of this occasion, one would have to admit that the signs included the people who received speaking in tongues. What other signs could have been present in the people being baptized in the Holy Spirit that so impressed the sorcerer that he would want to duplicate them? Would he want to reproduce a holy life? Would he want to replicate a dedication to the testimony of Jesus? Would he want to motivate a commitment to the gospel? I think not!

Obviously, Simon heard them speak with tongues and became enamored of the idea of how popular he could become and how much money he could gain if he could do the same as the apostles had done. We must admit that these Samaritans did speak with tongues. The practice was so consistent in the early church that Luke, the author of Acts, felt no need to specify the evidence.

Dr. F. F. Bruce contends,

> The context leaves us in no doubt that their receiving the Holy Spirit was attended by external manifestations such as had marked this descent on the earliest disciples at Pentecost.

A.T. Robertson, commenting on the Greek text, states that the language structure "shows plainly that those who received the gift of the Holy Spirit spoke with tongues." John Trapp the great Puritan scholar of the 17th century, commented, "The Holy Spirit fell upon the Samaritans in those extraordinary gifts of tongues and miracles."

Proof from Paul

Paul admitted he had been a religious zealot, a blasphemer and a persecutor of the early Christians (1 Timothy 1:13). However, God saw in him the qualities of a great champion of His gospel. While Paul was on his way to Damascus to arrest Christians and put them in prison, God appeared to him and caused him to be blind (Acts 9:3-8).

He then directed Paul to Damascus where God had prepared a Christian named Ananias to minister to him. For three days and nights, Paul fasted and prayed, waiting on God for further instructions. He received those instructions when Ananias "went his way, and entered into the house; and putting his hands on him said, Brother Saul, the Lord, even Jesus, that appeared unto thee in the way thou camest, hath sent me, that thou mightest receive thy sight, and be filled with the Holy Ghost"(v. 17).

Paul immediately received his sight, arose and was baptized in water. Even though the scriptures do not say so explicitly, Paul was obviously baptized with the Holy Spirit when Ananias laid hands on him and prayed for him. As Dr. Charles Conn aptly states:

> Following his conversion on the Damascus Road, Paul received the Holy Spirit when Ananias laid hands on him. Observe here that two things were to happen—Paul was to receive his sight, and he was to be filled with the Holy Ghost (v. 18). While we read that he indeed received his sight, it is not specified that he was filled with the Holy Ghost. Are we to gather then that he did not receive this impartation?

Admittedly, any such suggestion would be ridiculous. We know that he was filled with the Spirit, because Acts 13:9 says, "Then Saul, (who is also called Paul,) filled with the Holy Ghost, set his eyes on him." We follow with the same question regarding his speaking with tongues and arrive at the same answer. We cannot conclude that if Paul had spoken in tongues the scriptures would have clearly stated it.

The fact that Paul spoke in tongues when he received the baptism in the Holy Spirit is not recorded in the historic record. But his speaking in tongues is emphasized in the epistles with such statements as that of Paul who said, "I thank my God, I speak with tongues more than ye all" (1 Corinthians 14:18). Carl Brumback gives an accurate and reasonable observation:

> At the time Paul was writing the epistle of First Corinthians he possessed the gift of tongues (1 Corinthians 4:18). This being so, there must have been a first time when he was given this miracle of utterance. The logical place for the primary experience would have been, as in the case of all the other apostles, at the hour when he was filled with the Spirit.
>
> It is apparent that speaking with tongues was the accepted evidence of the baptism in the Holy Spirit among the apostles and the other brethren at Jerusalem. It is unthinkable that the chiefest of apostles could have received an experience that did not measure up to the standard.
>
> If Peter and his brethren found assurance in the speaking in tongues of friendly Gentiles, how great was the assurance which Ananias received upon hearing the arch-persecutor of the church speak with tongues just like the very saints against whom he had threatened and slaughtered.

The record of these two cases does not cast a negative shadow on speaking in tongues as the initial evidence of the Holy Spirit baptism. The circumstantial evidence presented here is as convincing as the evidence given in the record of tongues at Pentecost, Caesarea and Ephesus. They are beyond doubt, question or refutation. This gift is for you!

CHAPTER 4

ARE TONGUES THE ONLY EVIDENCE OF THE SPIRIT BAPTISM?

Again, the temptation to answer with only one word is strong. Although the answer is *no*, the matter is important and it deserves more attention than a one-word answer can give it. At the initial outpouring of the baptism in the Holy Spirit on the Day of Pentecost, there were three recognizable signs of the coming of the Holy Spirit:

- the sound of "a rushing mighty wind" (Acts 2:2);
- the appearance of "cloven tongues like as of fire" (v. 3), and
- all began to "speak with other tongues" (v. 4).

Please note that of the three signs, only the latter (speaking in tongues) has remained as the initial physical evidence of the baptism in the Holy Spirit. Donald Gee wrote:

> All the distinctive manifestations of the Day of Pentecost were not repeated and need not be expected. They are unnecessary. The Comforter has come and abides, but be it noted that enough is repeated to make subsequent Pentecost recognizable as such. The scriptures do not refer anymore to a rushing mighty wind, or cloven tongues of fire, but they do refer to speaking with tongues as the Spirit gives utterance.

William McDonald validates this emphasis:

> It is possible that the sound of the wind that attracted the first crowd on the Day of Pentecost had subsided and the fire had vanished before the mockers (Acts 2:13) arrived in the Upper Room, but the speaking with tongues remained as a 'sign' to them (Mark 16:17; 1 Corinthians 14:22). Significantly, tongues is repeated in other instances of the Spirit's outpouring throughout the Book of Acts, whenever the writer tells in detail what happens when people initially receive the Holy Spirit baptism. Speaking in tongues may well have been the norm in all the churches Paul founded, in that it was not such an uncommon thing that it had to be specified every time it occurred.

Dr. Ray H. Hughes accurately points out:

> Although we hold to the position of speaking with tongues as the initial evidence of the baptism in the Holy Spirit, by no means do we claim that this is the only evidence that one has been baptized in

the Holy Spirit. The Spirit does not come merely to speak, but the speaking is His announcement that He has come to the believer and will accompany him in performing the task of implementing the Great Commission. Speaking in tongues is not the zenith of the believer's experience, but a beginning of more effective service and a more powerful witnessing of Jesus Christ.

An appropriate analogy of our experience of the baptism in the Holy Spirit is that of electrical current that comes into our house or apartment. Simultaneously, it lights rooms, heats water for bathing and washing clothes, and freezes water into ice. Electricity runs the machine that blows cold air in the summer and warm air in the winter. It runs every electrical appliance in the house—from a small electric razor to a large washing machine loaded with clothes. There is only one electric current, but many and varied are the works it performs.

So it is with the baptism in the Holy Spirit. While He does, indeed, give utterance of speech to those whom He indwells, that is not, by any means, His primary function or purpose for coming to us. Sad, indeed, is the person who feels that the only function, or primary function, of the Holy Spirit's presence in his or her life is to speak with tongues.

That scenario can be compared to one sitting in total darkness in his house when he has electric current wired into it but does not know how to work the switch and turn on a light. Or, like a woman who feeds her family raw food because she doesn't know that electricity will make her stove hot enough to cook the food. Desiring to be baptized in the Holy Spirit only for the purpose of speaking with tongues misses the message of the Bible. Dr. Charles W. Conn wisely observes:

> We must take care not to attach undue significance to speaking with tongues. The phenomenon has a valid and proper place in the Christian experience, yet it is not an end in itself and should not be sought for its own sake. Tongues would be meaningless in themselves without the deeper Christian life they signify. They would be as meaningless as a herald for a king who does not live or as a marker for a place that does not exist. Tongues are a sign, a witness that accompanies the Holy Spirit when He comes into the heart of man. The phenomenon is the initial physical evidence that one has received the baptism in the Holy Spirit.

The work of the Holy Spirit is so vast and far-reaching that all of it cannot be covered in this short Book of Acts. However, I will mention a few in order to call attention to the many benefits of being filled with the Holy Spirit.

Jesus designated the Holy Spirit as our *teacher*:

> But the Comforter, which is the Holy Ghost, whom the Father will send in my name, he shall teach you all things, and bring all things to your remembrance, whatsoever I have said unto you (John 14:26; see also Nehemiah 9:20; Luke 12:12, 1 Corinthians 2:13, 1 John 2:27).

Paul shows that the Holy Spirit is our *intercessor and helper in prayer*: "For we know not what we should pray for as we ought: but the spirit itself maketh intercession for us with groanings which cannot be uttered" (Romans 8:26). He testified, "I will pray with the spirit, and I will pray with the understanding also" (1 Corinthians 14:15).

The Holy Spirit is our *abiding guest*: "And I will pray the Father, and He shall give you another Comforter, that He may abide with you for ever" (John 14:16).

Jesus designated Him to be our *guide*: "Howbeit, when He, the Spirit of truth, is come, He will guide you into all truth . . . He will shew you things to come" (John 16:13).

He is the *glorifier of Jesus*: "He shall glorify me"(v. 14).

Simon Peter stated that He is our *inspirer*: "For the prophecy came not in old time by the will of man: but holy men of God spake as they were moved by the Holy Ghost" (2 Peter 1:21).

He is our *empowerer*. "But ye shall receive power, after that the Holy Ghost is come upon you: and ye shall be witnesses unto me both in Jerusalem, and all Judea, and in Samaria, and unto the uttermost part of the earth" (Acts 1: 8). The scriptures designate Him as:

- The Spirit of promise (Ezekiel 36:27; Joel 2:28; Luke 24:8, 9; Galatians 3:14).
- The Spirit of truth (John 16:13)
- The Spirit of grace (Zechariah 12:10; Hebrews 10:29)

- The Spirit of life (Romans 8:2)
- The Spirit of adoption (Romans 8:15).

As we have seen, speaking in tongues is valid and is the initial evidence of the baptism in the Holy Spirit. However, we emphasize that certain other signs of the Holy Spirit indwelling a person are vital, important and convincing. Let us examine two of the other signs that are also requisite.

The Sign of a Changed Life

Nothing convinces the world that we have been filled with the Holy Spirit as much as a life of holiness that reflects a pure heart, a clean spirit and an attitude of love and sincerity. The devil can imitate tongues and the gifts of the Holy Spirit, but he cannot imitate a life of holiness.

Some react immediately and resist the mention of the word "holiness." They insist that it suggests legalism. Admittedly, there are occasions when legalistic teachings have been enforced in the name of holiness, but that is wrong and contrary to Scripture.

On the other hand, we must be careful that a distaste for legalism does not blind us to the reality of holiness, which God requires of His people in every age (Hebrews 12:14). The kind of holiness the Bible teaches is clear and unmistakable.

Paul described this holiness in his epistles to the churches. He makes a plea for a changed life that will bear the fruit of the indwelling Spirit. "But the fruit of the Spirit is love, joy, peace, long-suffering, gentleness, goodness, faith, Meekness, temperance: against such there is no law" (Galatians 5:22, 23). There is no legalism about those Christian graces, and seeing them in the life of a Spirit-filled Christian daily convinces the hardest of unbelievers.

Myer Pearlman makes a valid observation:

> Since the Holy Spirit does not work magically, but in a vital and progressive manner, it is by degrees that a soul is renewed. Faith must be strengthened through many tests; love must be fortified to survive hardship and temptations. Allurements to sin must be overcome; tendencies and habits must be corrected.

Before conversion, we practiced sin daily and programmed ourselves to react and respond to certain stimuli and situations in life; after conversion we must practice holiness. Paul gives explicit directions about how to accomplish this: "I beseech you therefore, brethren, by the mercies of God, that ye present your bodies a living sacrifice, holy, acceptable unto God, which is your reasonable service" (Romans 12:1).

He calls on us to see ourselves as dead to sin: "Likewise reckon ye also yourselves to be dead indeed unto sin, but alive unto God through Jesus Christ our Lord" (Romans 6:11). Consider the analogy of a confirmed alcoholic. The man spends everything on drink; he lives to get drunk again. Then, on day he dies! You could roll his body into a warehouse filled with every kind of alcoholic beverage, leave him for a week and he would single bottle of the beverage. He's dead! He could never resist a drink while he was alive, but now he is not even aware of its presence.

This is the kind of crucifixion to the desires of the flesh that Paul is pleading for in the followers of Jesus. He concludes, "How shall we that are dead to sin, live any longer therein?" (Romans 6:2). He also warns, "For if ye live after the flesh, ye shall die: but if ye through the Spirit do mortify the deeds of the body, ye shall live" (Romans 8:13).

Dr. Charles W. Conn admonishes us that "hardness is not holiness." At this point we must be cautious. There seems to be a general tendency in the Christian community to insist on holy living; but in attempting to enforce conformity, some become hard—even harsh. This can be especially true with pastors, teachers or church leaders.

Two words the Bible uses to designate ministers or pastors with oversight of a group of people are *servant* (Matthew 20:27; 23:11) and *shepherd* (Jeremiah 23:4; Acts 20:28, *NIV*). Both have a connotation of gentleness, meekness and respect. We must make a careful effort to avoid teaching personal likes and dislikes, as well as personal convictions, as divine requirements under the guise of holiness. This practice of the scribes and Pharisees was strongly condemned by the Lord Jesus (Matthew 13:13-23).

Certainly, we desire our congregation and members to exhibit Christian virtues and to live by a holy standard. We have a right to expect this. But we must also remember that abstinence from anything, just for the sake of conformity, is not holiness. Keeping a cold set of rules and catechisms or observing a particular occasion is neither holiness nor Christianity.

Some feel that the stricter the rules, the greater the degree of holiness. Jesus did not emphasize keeping rules; He taught principles for living—which, in turn, produced holy lives. The Holy Spirit enables us and motivates us to live holy lives before God (see Romans 12:1; Hebrews 12:14).

Some respected teachers contend that the dedicated work of one who has been baptized with the Holy Spirit is the most important and vital evidence of the Spirit's indwelling a person. It is difficult if not impossible to prioritize or place the importance of one outward evidence above another.

The ideal example is a balanced life that produces all of the outward evidence of the Holy Spirit's indwelling and control of a person. The Bible teaches clearly that speaking in tongues is the "initial" evidence of the baptism with the Holy Spirit, and that it occurs immediately upon reception. But a holy life lived daily will be a subsequent outward evidence, as will a life of dedicated and effective service.

There is no need to list all the evidences in a particular order or sequence since they are involved with and include other signs of the Holy Spirit baptism (Mark 16:17, 18). Casting out demons, healing the sick and working of miracles were results of the early disciples' receiving the baptism in the Holy Spirit, and is evident in the Bible account of the early church.

The Sign of Dedicated, Effective Service

Another outward evidence of the indwelling of the Holy Spirit is dedicated and effective witnessing and ministry. Before Jesus' Ascension, He gave His followers a promise of the Holy Spirit baptism: "But ye shall receive power, after that the Holy Ghost is come upon you: and ye shall be witnesses unto me both in Jerusalem, and all Judea, and in Samaria, and unto the uttermost part of the earth" (Acts 1:8).

Preoccupied with thoughts about Christ restoring the kingdom to Israel, the disciples had just asked Him if He was going to do so at that time (v. 6). Jesus emphasized to them that this was not their primary concern (v. 7). Before time was spent and energy exerted planning for kingdom restoration, there was something more pertinent, more important and more pressing.

This was the carrying out of the Great Commission: "Go ye into all the world, and preach the gospel" (Mark 16:15).

To equip them for that global task, Jesus promised the gift of the Holy Spirit baptism: "For John truly baptized with water; but ye shall be baptized with the Holy Ghost not many days hence" (Acts 1:5). They received that baptism 10 days later in the Upper Room.

In verse 8, Jesus emphasized an enduement of power they would need in order to carry out the commission of reaching the world with the gospel. He indicated the results of the enduement: "And ye shall be witnesses unto me" (v. 8). This particular outward evidence of the baptism in the Holy Spirit seems to have been predominant in the early church after the Day of Pentecost.

Beginning with the worship service in the Upper Room where 120 were baptized with the Holy Spirit, effective evangelism and soul winning were set in motion. This became the standard for the early church.

Peter stood with the other apostles to defend the 120 who received the infilling of the Holy Spirit (Acts 2:14). He told what the occasion was not: "For these are not drunken, as ye suppose" (v. 15). Then he proclaimed what it was: "This is that which was spoken by the prophet Joel" (v. 16). Peter then proceeded to connect the occurrence with Jesus Christ, "Therefore let all the house of Israel know assuredly, that God hath made that same Jesus, whom ye have crucified, both Lord and Christ" (v. 36).

His message brought conviction to the people and evangelism was set in motion.

> Now when they heard this, they were pricked in their heart, and said unto Peter and to the rest of the apostles, Men and brethren, what shall we do? Then Peter said unto them, Repent and be baptized every one of you in the name of Jesus Christ for the remission of sins, and ye shall receive the

> gift of the Holy Ghost. . . . Then they that gladly received his word were baptized: and the same day there were added unto them about three thousand souls (vv. 37, 41).

What a dramatic start for the young church. It was victory at the outset! Three thousand converts joined the church in the very first service! But this was only the beginning:

> And they, continuing daily with one accord in the temple, and breaking bread from house to house, did eat their meat with gladness and singleness of heart, praising God and having favor with all the people. And the Lord added to the church daily such as should be saved (vv. 46, 47).

Effective evangelism and soul winning were daily occurrences after the Day of Pentecost and the infilling of the Holy Spirit. The daily activities of the early church produced opportunities to witness for Jesus. This brought persecution, created controversy and opened even more doors of opportunity to do the work of the church.

An example is Acts 3. Peter and John were going to the temple to pray (obviously a daily practice), when they encountered a man lying at the gate to the temple. He had been lame all his life (v. 2). The apostles engaged the man in conversation and told him, "We don't have money to give you, but we can give you something money can't buy. In the name of Jesus, get up and walk" (v. 6, paraphrase).

This brought about the arrest of Peter and John, but that only opened the door of opportunity for them to witness and preach Christ to the Jewish leaders who arrested them (vv. 12-26). After they were imprisoned the second time, they had the opportunity to witness and preach to many and to see great results, "Howbeit many of them which heard the word believed; and the number of the men was about five thousand" (4:4).

Acts 5 tells of the miraculous healings by the apostles which brought "a multitude out of the cities round about unto Jerusalem, bringing sick folks, and them which were vexed with unclean spirits: and they were healed every one" (5:16). The phenomenal results continued when "believers were the more added to the Lord, multitudes both of men and women" (v. 14).

I believe this pattern of operation and results should be experienced by every Christian church today. In Acts 6, the first seven deacons of the Christian church were selected. The qualifications were set forth by the apostles. They were to be "of honest report, full of the Holy Ghost and wisdom" (v. 3). Can we afford to have lesser qualifications for the lay leaders in our churches today?

One of the deacons, Stephen, became the first martyr of the church. Another, Philip, had a citywide revival in Samaria and hundreds accepted Jesus as Savior (8:6).

> Unclean spirits, crying with loud voice, came out of many that were possessed with them; and many taken with palsies, and that were lame, were healed. And there was great joy in that city" (vv. 7, 8).

After the great citywide revival in Samaria, the Spirit directed Philip into the desert to witness to an Ethiopian official of Queen Candace (vv. 26-40). It should be pointed out that Philip's ministry to one man in the desert was as important and successful as if it was in the city of Samaria. Luke reported, "And the people with one accord gave heed unto those things which Philip spake" (8:6). We know that 100 percent of Philip's congregation in the desert responded by accepting Christ and being baptized in water (vv. 36-38)!

With our commendable efforts of mass evangelism, we must not overlook the individual witness. The world is populated one at a time, and heaven will be populated when men and women are born again one at a time. In Acts, it is apparent that revival and evangelism, both mass and personal, were characteristics of the early church.

Any church baptized in the Holy Spirit can expect the same results today—corporately *and* in the lives of individuals. We must be baptized in the Holy Spirit according to the Biblical pattern.

Speaking with tongues is the initial, physical evidence of being baptized in the Holy Spirit, but it is not the only evidence. Nor is it the primary purpose of Holy Spirit baptism. When our experience is consistent with the Scriptural directives given in this chapter, we will constantly produce the fruit and works of the Holy Spirit who indwells our lives.

CHAPTER 5

The Gifts of the Holy Spirit

The *gift of the Spirit*, and the *gifts of the Spirit* are two entirely different subjects in this study. In the singular use of *gift*, we refer to the experience of the baptism in the Holy Spirit. In the plural use of *gifts*, we refer to the gifts of the Holy Spirit which Paul enumerated in 1 Corinthians 12:8-10:

> For to one is given by the Spirit the word of wisdom; to another the word of knowledge by the same Spirit; to another faith by the same Spirit; to another the gifts of healing by the same Spirit; to another the working of miracles; to another prophecy; to another discerning of spirits; to another divers kinds of tongues; to another the interpretation of tongues.

The *gifts* of the Spirit are available only to those who have received *the gift* of the Holy Spirit. The baptism in the Holy Spirit is a prerequisite for all who desire the best gifts (see 1 Corinthians 12:31, *NKJV*). Since the Holy Spirit is the administrator of all the gifts (v. 4), and they are operated at His discretion (v. 11), it follows that His indwelling of a person is the first necessity.

The gifts of the Spirit operating in the church today is as controversial as the baptism in the Holy Spirit with the initial evidence of speaking in tongues. Generally, the same people object to both.

This is normal, I suppose, since one is the product of the other. But the people in need of help and to whom the church should be ministering are the ultimate losers from these objections or restrictions. I repeat: The baptism in the Holy Spirit is prerequisite to having access to the gifts of the Spirit.

When I was teaching on this subject in a pastors seminar, a young minister approached me with the question, "What do I have to do to get the gifts of the Spirit?" I replied to him, "First, I must know why you desire the gifts and then I can answer you." He proceeded to tell me that he wanted to be known as a spiritual preacher who is close to God, and that he wanted everyone for whom he prayed to be healed.

As he talked I did not hear a single statement revealing the right reasons for wanting the gifts. I startled him when I told him that I doubted he would be having any of the gifts in his ministry because he seemed to want them primarily to focus attention on himself and to make him popular.

That is the reason Simon the sorcerer used when he offered money to Peter and John who had laid hands on the people in Samaria and they received the gift of the Holy Spirit.

> When Simon saw that through laying on of the apostlesí hands the Holy Ghost was given, he offered them money, saying, íGive me also this power, that on whomsoever I lay hands, he may receive the Holy Ghostî (Acts 8:18, 19).

Like the rich young ruler in the Bible, the young man went away sorrowfully. I tried to be tactful in what I said to him, but the truth both shocked and disappointed him.

The Spirit Uses His Gifts for His Purpose

Paul showed that God, who gave the baptism in the Holy Spirit (John 14:16), set administrations and gifts in the church by the Holy Spirit: "And God hath set some in the church, first apostles, secondarily prophets, thirdly teachers" (1 Corinthians 12:28). The Holy Spirit uses these administrations to work His purposes in the church.

He has also set gifts in the church by the Holy Spirit: the word of wisdom, the word of knowledge, faith, healing, working of miracles, prophecy, discerning of spirits, divers kinds of tongues, and interpretation of tongues (see vv. 8-10).

God did not place the offices of pastor, prophet and teacher in the church to elevate men above their fellows so that they could be served by others. He placed them there for men and women who will lead the church in spiritual integrity, bless the church by bearing the fruit of the Spirit (Galatians 5:22-24), and display Christian graces and the gifts of the Spirit in their lives daily.

Both the administrations and spiritual gifts were set in the church for blessing and up-building the saints, and for expanding the kingdom. They are never solely for the benefit of the individuals who operate them.

Jesus himself would not yield to the temptation of the devil in the wilderness to "command this stone that it be made bread," because His power was to be used only for the glory of God (see Luke 4:1-4). Paul warns: "Let us not be desirous of vain glory" (Galatians 5:26).

He exhorted us to "covet earnestly the best gifts" (1 Corinthians 12:31). Paul did not specify what the "best gifts" are. He may not have felt it necessary because he showed the answer in the context of 1 Corinthians 12–14. There he summarized the purpose of all the gifts: "Let all things be done unto edifying" (14:26).

The Holy Spirit cannot and will not do His work through ulterior or carnal motives. "For God is not the author of confusion, but of peace" (v. 33).

When Jesus used His power of healing or miracles in His earthly ministry, it was in response to the compassion He felt for the people to whom He ministered. "I have compassion on the multitude" (Matthew 15:32). "He was moved with compassion on them, because they fainted" (9:36). "When the Lord saw her, he had compassion on her" (Luke 7:13).

The desire to help others and minister to their needs is the underlying principle in the use of the spiritual gifts. No spiritual gift is the personal property of an individual. Much error and abuse have resulted from not understanding this cardinal truth.

We would do well to heed the declaration of Dr. Ray H. Hughes: "All of the spiritual gifts are resident in the Holy Spirit, and when one is full of the Holy Spirit, he has the potential of all the gifts of the Spirit."

The Spirit Distributes His Gifts As He Wills

God distributes the gifts of the Spirit, but not as we sometimes give gifts to family at Christmas. He has never wrapped the gift of healing, for example, in a pretty gift box and then given it to an individual to use at his or her discretion or will. He also determines the operation of the gifts.

The Reverend Bennie Triplett maintains: "These gifts are dispensed by the Holy Spirit (see 1 Corinthians 12:11). They are not natural talents.

They are neither purchased, merited nor deserved. They are disbursed freely by the Holy Spirit, 'to every man . . . as He will.'"

When one is baptized in the Holy Spirit, he will go about his ministry daily in a natural manner as necessity dictates—not planning anything spectacular or dramatic but desiring only to minister to all and to be God's instrument. As he encounters various situations which require a power he does not have naturally, the Holy Spirit, residing within, dispenses one of the spiritual gifts—or all nine of them, if necessary—to enable him to minister competently and effectively.

There is a constant flow of Holy Spirit power and activity in the life and ministry of those who are dedicated to the work and will of God, both ministers and laymen. It is incorrect to say that an individual has the gift of prophecy or gift of tongues—or any of the gifts, for that matter.

I emphasize the fact that everyone who has the baptism in the Holy Spirit has within the potential manifestation and working of any one or all nine of the gifts of the Holy Spirit. The gifts of the Spirit have never been, and will never be, the possession of an individual, however holy that person may appear. It was true of the apostles, and it has been true of every Christian since.

A timely and classic example is described in Acts 5. Shortly after the Day of Pentecost, the early church members so reacted to the joy and exuberance of their newfound experience that

> the multitude of them that believed were of one heart and of one soul: neither said any of them that ought of the things which he possessed was his own; but they had all things common. Neither was there any among them that lacked: for as many as were possessors of lands or houses sold them, and brought the prices of the things that were sold, and laid them down at the apostles' feet: and distribution was made unto every man according as he had need (Acts 4:32, 34, 35).

While most of the local members were doing this, one couple—Ananias and Sapphira—wanted to appear as generous and loving as others, but apparently had not experienced the same degree of emotional excitement as the others. The couple conspired to sell a possession (5:1, 2) and to keep back part of the price.

They were under no obligation to sell any of their possessions or give any of the proceeds after they had sold it, so their sole intent was to deceive and be untruthful.

They planned for the husband to go first, taking a part of the proceeds of the sale and giving it to the apostles. He told the church that this was the total price of the sale. His wife went later and confirmed the amount her husband had said.

They failed to take into account the fact that they would be dealing with a church leader who was "filled with the Holy Ghost" (4:8). He would be the channel for the Holy Spirit to operate at least five of the nine spiritual gifts listed in 1 Corinthians 12, in order to expose their conspiracy and hypocrisy. In Luke's account of the scenario, the Holy Spirit flowed smoothly and promptly to enable Simon Peter to handle the situation effectively.

> But Peter said, "Ananias, why hath Satan filled thine heart to lie to the Holy Ghost [the gift of discernment], and to keep back part of the price of the land [the gift of knowledge]? Whiles it remained, was it not thine own? and after it was sold, was it not in thine own power? why hast thou conceived this thing in thine heart? thou hast not lied unto men, but unto God [gift of wisdom]." And Ananias hearing these words fell down, and gave up the ghost [gift of miracles]: and great fear came on all them that heard these things. And the young men arose, wound him up and carried him out, and buried him (Acts 5:3-6).

In this part of the episode, we see the apostle Peter operate four different gifts: discernment, knowledge, wisdom and miracles. In the remaining part we see those same four repeated along with a fifth one.

The Spirit Operates His Gifts in His People

> And it was about the space of three hours after, when his wife, not knowing what was done, came in. And Peter answered unto her, "Tell me whether ye sold the land for so much?" [wisdom]. And she said, "Yea,

for so much." Then Peter said unto her, "How is it that ye have agreed together [knowledge] to tempt the Spirit of the Lord? [discernment] behold, the feet of them which have buried thy husband are at the door, and shall carry thee out" [prophecy]. Then she fell down straightway at his feet, and yielded up the ghost [miracles]: and the young men came in, and found her dead, and, carrying her forth, buried her by her husband (vv. 7-10).

The Bible clearly shows the scriptural plan for the operation of the nine spiritual gifts. Although five of the nine gifts were operated by the apostle Peter here, it could not be said accurately that he had the gift of discernment, the gift of wisdom, the gift of knowledge, the gift of miracles or the gift of prophecy. The Holy Spirit who indwelt Peter enabled him to operate these five gifts because the situation required them.

Peter knew nothing beforehand about what would transpire that day. He had not planned it, rehearsed it, or known that it would happen. He was merely taking care of this business as the leader of the church at Jerusalem at that time. Having received the baptism in the Holy Spirit previously, he was prepared and equipped to deal effectively with any situation that might arise.

He could have employed the other four gifts of the Spirit had the occasion called for them. Notice the smooth flow of those four gifts in the entire episode. There was no preplanned starting of one, no sudden stops or the sudden starting of another. Since they were being administered by the Holy Spirit, the gifts supported one another, reinforced one another, overlapped one another, and confirmed one another in a smooth flow of the Holy Spirit's anointing power in the life and ministry of Peter.

The effect of this dramatic display of God's power had a positive effect on both the church and community.

> And great fear came upon all the church, and upon as many as heard these things. And believers were the more added to the Lord, multitudes both of men and women (vv. 11, 14).

The gifts of the Spirit should operate the same way in the churches of today. We do not have to resort to fabricated miracles, trickery, spiritual excesses or spiritual abuses.

"Jesus Christ the same yesterday, and to day, and for ever" (Hebrews 13:8).

"For the promise [gift] is unto you, and to your children, and to all that are afar off, even as many as the Lord our God shall call" (Acts 2:39).

CHAPTER 6

Was Speaking in Tongues for Apostles Only?

Critics and opponents of the Pentecostal experience want you to believe that the Holy Spirit baptism and speaking with tongues were just for apostolic times. They teach that the experience and blessings were only for the early church, and that all happenings of the experience ceased with the passing of the apostles. If such were the case there would unquestionably be conclusive evidence of it.

But where is the evidence? Who has ever produced even a thread of support for such teaching? In fact, all evidence proves the opposite. Some objections to the baptism in the Holy Spirit with the evidence of speaking with tongues are reinforced by the position of church denominations, which is a flimsy shield at best. Church history reveals that when the church becomes cold, formal, ritualistic and a pawn of governments, God sends radical revivalists to awaken the church and call people to repentance and reformation. These revival leaders are often rejected, ridiculed and scorned by established church leaders who are disturbed and embarrassed by revival results.

Pentecost came at such a time in church history, and it provoked the opposition and persecution described in the Book of Acts. Throughout the history of the church, demonstrations and reoccurrences of the baptism in the Holy Spirit have spawned opposition and rejection by the hierarchy and powers that be of the established churches—who themselves had failed to perpetuate the doctrine and experience of Pentecost.

But the fact that the experience and practice of Holy Spirit baptism has been so ardently opposed and suppressed by church leaders through history seems to verify its validity. Attempts to suppress or deny the experience only makes it more popular and whet the spiritual appetite of those who want to know more about the experience and why the vehement denunciation of it. After learning more about the experience, many come to embrace it and receive its blessings and joy.

When suppression, denial, rejection and persecution failed to cause the experience to be filed away and forgotten, attempts to discredit both the teachers of the Pentecostal experience and those who received it became the order of the day. Still the Pentecostals would not go away. Their numbers kept growing. Their followers kept increasing. The Pentecostal experience spread further than ever before.

Documented evidence verifies that in every century since Pentecost, the baptism in the Holy Spirit with the initial evidence of speaking in tongues has been present in the church. I will present only a small sampling of that evidence, but it will be sufficient for the honest heart to be convinced of the reality of this experience. The dishonest heart will never be convinced.

Dr. R. Leonard Carroll shared his experience of a scholarly search for evidence:

> To trace the recurrence of tongues speaking through the centuries is a most enlightening experience. An elementary observation, however, reveals that it is a mistaken assertion that the manifestation of glossolalia completely disappeared shortly after the Day of Pentecost. The facts of church history, on the other hand, reveal that this concept, for the most part has been based upon a deliberate and structured effort to circumvent tongues speaking, or the concept was erected upon stark ignorance. But it is profitable to review the annals of man for historical evidence which relate to the miracle of speaking in tongues. It is clearly evident that many times since Pentecost, speaking with tongues has broken out

of its institutional container—the church—and has reworked the religious landscape.

The *Interpreter's Dictionary of the Bible* states, "Through the centuries glossolalia has frequently reappeared among Christian groups."

G. B. Cutten wrote: "Many isolated examples of speaking with tongues might be given, extending down through the ages. . . . In most cases, the appearance of speaking with tongues has been connected with revival experiences."

The *Encyclopedia Britannica* asserts that miraculous utterances recur in Christian revivals in every age. Lefferts A. Loetscher is clear and emphatic in his statement: "The phenomenon of 'speaking with tongues as the Spirit gives utterance' (Acts 2:1-13) has appeared in all ages of the Church."

Dr. Phillip Schaff, universally acknowledged historian, has won the acclaim of all discerning scholars. He wrote, "The speaking with tongues, however, was not confined to the Day of Pentecost. . . . This gift perpetuated itself. We find traces of it still in the second and third centuries."

John E. Steinmueller and Kathryn Sullivan make this comment in the *Catholic Biblical Encyclopedia*: "In regard to the perpetuation of these charisms, it may be said that, although they were manifested more frequently in the infant Church and the first few centuries, they have never been completely lacking in the Church."

Eusebius of Caesarea (AD 260-340), the "father of church history," gave a rather sarcastic account of a sect which practiced speaking with tongues. The sarcasm focused, however, on the fact that glossolalia was indeed practiced in the church at that particular time in history. That some got out of order in their conduct does not reflect on the significance of the practice, not negate its place in Biblical teaching.

No honest Pentecostal today would deny the existence of abuses and excesses, but they do not represent the Pentecostal Movement. Nor do they negate the reality and validity of the vast majority of Pentecostals who are above reproach and uphold the standard of righteousness that God expects of people who have been born again and are indwelled by the Holy Spirit.

Who would deny that unscrupulous and incapable doctors practice medicine in every country; but no sane person rejects the vast majority of doctors who are men and women of integrity and dedication, and who are skilled and trained to relieve suffering. The same can be said of every profession and of religion.

When God sent Moses to Pharaoh to plead for the release of the Israelites from Egyptian bondage and slavery, He enabled Moses to work a miracle before Pharaoh. He told Aaron to throw down his rod, and it became a serpent. Pharaoh then called his magicians who threw down their rods, which also became serpents (see Exodus 7:10-13). The devil has always been able to imitate God's work, but there is always a criteria that reveals one to be the genuine work of God and the other to be a fabrication of something sinister and cheap.

When the Egyptian magicians' rods became serpents, immediately Aaron's rod swallowed them up. That gave unmistakable evidence which miracle was of God and which was of man. Usually, even unregenerate persons can detect the imitation of speaking with tongues or the imitation of the gifts of the Spirit. Such displays give evidence like Paul's "sounding brass, or a tinkling cymbal" (1 Corinthians 13:1).

To further document the evidence that speaking with tongues is a fact of history from Pentecost until the Reformation, let's look at Tertullian (AD 150-230), a North African church leader of unquestioned repute. He stated:

> The apostle most assuredly foretold that there were to be "spiritual gifts" in the church. Now, can you refuse to believe this, even if indubitable evidence on every point is forthcoming for your conviction?

Basil the Great was a distinguished church teacher of the fourth century. He consigned the gifts of the Spirit, including diversities of tongues, to the arranging of the church. He said the church was the designated container of the gifts of the Holy Spirit. Leo the Great stated in a sermon:

> While the days of Pentecost were fulfilled and all the disciples were together in the same place, there occurred suddenly from heaven a sound as of a violent wind coming, and filled the whole house where they were sitting. And there appeared to them divided tongues as of fire, and it sat upon each of them. And they were all filled with the Holy Spirit, and began to speak with other tongues, as the Holy Spirit gave them utterance. . . . No interpretation is required for understanding, no practice for using, no time for studying, but the Spirit of Truth blowing where He wills, the languages peculiar to each nation became common property in the mouth of the Church. . . . From that day the showers of gracious gifts, the rivers of blessings, have watered every desert and all the dry land.

To list all of the many documentations which Dr. Leonard Carroll researched would be boring or laborious. But these sufficient, valid and trustworthy records show unquestionably that the practice of speaking in tongues by Spirit-filled Christians was a perpetual practice through history.

The facts completely discredit and refute the contention that speaking in tongues passed away with the apostles in the early church. Dr. Carroll's valid questions demands an answer from critics of speaking in tongues today:

> Can it be assumed that tongues speaking was simply to give the Early Church a triumphant entree into a hostile world? If the church needed such a unique and heavenly manifestation to begin an effective ministry, would it not be reasonable to

reckon how desperately the church needed such a phenomenon in order to maintain a meaningful and continuing service to Christ within the confines of an increasingly sinful and contrary world?

Would a just God equip one age of His church more adequately than He would the succeeding ages? I think not!

In the Reformation God raised up noble men to reform an apostate church. Since Pentecost, the church had strayed from the fervency and dedication of the early church. Zeal to evangelize was channeled into political efforts and the promotion of social issues of the time. Commitment to the Great Commission to "go ye into all the world, and preach the gospel to every creature" (Mark 16:15) had deteriorated. Men went to heathen countries, not to convert the citizens from their pagan practices, but, in some instances, to incorporate pagan rites into the Christian form of worship.

In many countries the church had become a pawn of the government and the clergy had become government agents. The apostles' doctrine had been replaced generally and made into catechisms so that public worship had come to consist of a system of rituals with cold formality.

The Reformation had its unplanned beginning when a young German monk named Martin Luther was stirred and challenged as the Holy Spirit burned into his heart the neglected teaching of the early church that a man is justified by faith.

This dedicated servant of God became the object of rejection, ridicule and scorn. He was excommunicated from his church and cut off from almost all that had been dear to him. But he had heard from heaven, and knew that he had a mandate from a power greater than the church! The Reformation was born.

Through the next two centuries God raised up other great men who, like Luther, burned with a passion to be used of the Holy Spirit to bring revival to the church of Jesus Christ. They witnessed and lived to restore doctrinal orthodoxy, holy living and spiritual fervor to the church.

There was no preplanned interaction or communication between the Reformation leaders. Nor were there any organized efforts among their strategies and works. The Holy Spirit obviously called each of them individually and commissioned them to do their respective works. Their efforts fit together like pieces in a puzzle, revealing God's overall plan to restore His church to its original purpose and power.

Significantly, during the Reformation the leaders recognized and acknowledged the Pentecostal power and the practice of speaking with tongues as the Spirit gave utterance.

According to Souer's writings of the Christian church, "Dr. Martin Luther was a . . . speaker in tongues and interpreter . . . endowed with all the gifts of the Holy Spirit." When Luther was asked about the phenomenon that occurred on the Day of Pentecost, he replied:

> They could speak diverse languages.... This was one of the greatest miracles that ever happened, that poor fishermen should receive such splendid gifts. It is just as if I were to awaken a stone and make it talk in all manner of languages.

It is evident that the practice of speaking in tongues was never completely removed from the church. From its inception at Pentecost through the great Reformation, we have documented its presence in that segment of the church where revival fervency, obedience to God and hunger for God were prominent. It was seldom practiced where coldness, ritual and formality dominated.

Bennie Triplett aptly stated:

> God, the Holy Spirit has always been involved in manís existence. Directly and indirectly He executes the design of God on this earth. The basic instrument through which He works is man. The agency with which He works is the church. The guidebook by which He works is the Bible. And neither are we to think that speaking with tongues passed away with the Reformers any more than it did with the passing of the apostles after the Day of Pentecost.

Since the Reformation the practice of speaking in tongues has increased significantly. Today, the Pentecostal experience has become so widespread throughout the world, the Pentecostal Movement is commonly referred to as the "third force" in the Christian church. The constituency of many Pentecostal churches is made up predominantly of former members of Catholic and "traditional" Protestant churches who yearned passionately for a deeper experience with God.

John Calvin, the Swiss reformer, says of the Spirit's speaking: "The meaning is now obvious. If, therefore, I frame prayers in a language that is not understood by me, and the Spirit supplies me with words, the Spirit indeed itself, which regulates my tongue, will in that case pray."

In referring to tongues Calvin commented about theologians who disdained them:

> At present great theologians . . . declaim against them [the use of tongues] with furious zeal. And it is certain, that the Holy Spirit has here honoured the use of tongues with never-dying praise, we may very readily gather, what is the kind of spirit that actuates these reformers, who level as many reproaches as they can against the pursuit of them. . . . Paul, nevertheless, commends the use of tongues. So far is he from wishing them abolished or thrown away.

David Smith, Scottish Presbyterian professor, quoted Bruey on the Huguenots of the Cevennes:

> The most striking instances of the gift of tongues in modern times are the 'little prophets of Cevennes' at the close of the 17th century and the Irvingites early in the 19th; and it is remarkable that these exhibited respectively the phenomenon of the Day

of Pentecost as portrayed in the Book of Acts and the ecstasies which convulsed the Corinthian Church . . . they preached and exhorted, not in the Romance patois of their native mountains, but in good French.

Welshman Matthew Henry (1662–1714), who pastored a Presbyterian church for 25 years, writes regarding tongues:

They began to speak in other tongues, besides their native language, though they had never learned any other. They spoke not matters of common conversation, but the word of God, and the praises of his name, as the Spirit gave them utterance . . . apophthegms, substantial and weighty sayings . . . It is probable that it was not only one that was enabled to speak one language, and another . . . but that every one was enabled to speak divers languages, as he would have occasion to use them. . . .

They did not speak here a word of another tongue, or stammer out some broken sentences, but spoke it as readily, properly, and elegantly, as if it had been their mother-tongue; for whatever was produced by miracle was the best of the kind. . . . Now this was . . . a very great miracle . . . They had not only never learned these languages, but had never learned any foreign tongue . . . They were neither scholars nor travellers.

John Wesley, the great preacher and founder of the Methodist Church (1703-1791), defines tongues as a sign to unbelievers "to engage their attention, and convince them the message is of God."

Jacob Baumgarten, German theologian, states: "The Christians, in consequence of having received the gift of the Spirit, spake with other tongues. . . . This expression might, possibly, convey . . . that 'the tongues of the disciples were essentially changed by the operation of the Spirit, and now became the organs of the Holy Ghost, whereas they had formerly been the organs of flesh.'"

The spirit of revival so swept the world in the 19th century that it would be difficult to chronicle the instances of the Holy Spirit baptism and the subsequent speaking in tongues. The practice became so commonplace that in some areas it was the expected rather than the exception.

During this same time England, France, Scotland, Germany and other countries of Europe experienced revival fires reminiscent of the church after the Day of Pentecost. In America, the revival surge was swept across the nation from shore to shore. Crowds of 30,000 to 50,000 would regularly attend a single service in outdoor stadiums.

Significantly, these revivals were marked by the presence of the Holy Spirit baptism which transcended denominational barriers and overcame diverse cultures and customs.

President Arnold T. Olson, Evangelical Free Church of America, writes:

> Believing as we do in the presence and power of the Holy Spirit we must accept the possibility and

probability of spiritual manifestations. But each and all of these must be in accord with the Word of God, whether they be tongues, renewals, revivals, or infillings. To deny the possibility of the Holy Spirit speaking through a believer in an 'unknown tongue' would be to limit the power of the third Person of the Godhead.

F. F. Bruce, distinguished English scholar and professor of Biblical history, compares the present-day church to the early church. He says:

> Speaking with tongues, or glossolalia (to give the phenomenon its Greek name), is not an unparalleled manifestation. Not only are the speaker's words partially or completely beyond his conscious control, but they are uttered in a language of which he has no command in normal circumstances.

Henry P. Van Dusen, past president of Union Theological Seminary in New York, states:

> The Pentecostal movement is nothing less than a revolution comparable in importance to the establishment of the original apostolic church and to the Protestant Reformation.

The Living Church, an independent Episcopal weekly, wrote about glossolalia (July 17, 1960):

> Speaking in tongues is no longer a phenomenon of some odd sect across the street. It is in our midst, and it is being practiced by clergy and laity who have stature and good reputation in the Church . . . Its widespread introduction would jar against our esthetic sense and some of our more strongly entrenched preconceptions."

The Reverend Bennie Triplett said:

> Neo-Pentecostalism is a term that is used to define glossolalists who attend the historic churches. This new movement has spread rapidly throughout most nominal and traditional churches. It has its basis primarily in tongues speaking. Groups and individuals are found in the Catholic, Lutheran, Episcopal, Presbyterian, Methodist, Baptist, Greek Orthodox and other denominations. They are also active in such universities, colleges and seminaries as Yale, Princeton, Notre Dame and Asbury. It is not uncommon today for a headline to read, "Speaking in Tongues Spreading to Most Denominations." The *Baptist and Reflector* declared, "The new Pentecost is not limited to Pentecostal sects. It has leaped all boundaries." Some neo-Pentecostals do not wish to leave their existing churches in preference to a Pentecostal church. The traditional churches have been forced to adjust in order to retain these people. Some have made allowances, while others have excommunicated or barred those who speak in tongues.

The irrefutable evidence from the Bible, clearly given in this book, validates the experience of the baptism in the Holy Spirit and the initial outward evidence of speaking with tongues.

Accepting these truths, you are faced with an imposing decision. Will you continue to be led by church leaders who refuse to accept the clear teaching of the Bible?

Will you stifle your hunger for more of God in your life and deny your soul to be indwelt by the fullness of the Holy Spirit, perhaps for the sake of social status or to follow the tradition of your denomination or family?

Or will you do as millions around the world have done: follow your heart which yearns to experience a deeper walk with God and a greater degree of spiritual power in your life and ministry.

You can experience a new level of victory over the weaknesses of life that discourage you. They cause you to despair, or to question the validity of God's requirements for His people to live a holy life. Jesus declared emphatically, "Ye shall receive power, after that the Holy Ghost is come upon you" (Acts 1:8).

I join the apostle Peter in assuring you that "the promise [gift] is unto you, and to your children, and to all that are afar off, even as many as the Lord our God shall call" (Acts 2:39).

Be honest with yourself. What are your objections to the baptism in the Holy Spirit with the initial outward evidence of speaking in tongues? Are they really based on the Word of God, or on the position of a church leader?

Can you prove by the Bible, without distorting or rationalizing it, that the Holy Spirit baptism and speaking in tongues are not for people of today? Can you effectively and conclusively prove by the Bible, history or any other method that the experience passed away with the original apostles?

Some object on the basis that they do not understand all the Bible teachings on the Holy Spirit baptism and speaking in tongues. I relate to them because after 53 years of enjoying the baptism in the Holy Spirit and speaking in tongues, I confess I do not fully understand every detail of the experience. But I can testify to the reality and blessings of this heavenly experience.

Have people of any era comprehended and understood all of God? Most of the things we enjoy are those we do not understand or comprehend; but we continue to enjoy their benefits. I do not understand how a black cow can eat green grass and give white milk and yellow butter, but that does not prevent me from drinking the milk, spreading the butter on my bread or eating the beef when the cow is slaughtered and processed.

We should take God's promises at face value even if we cannot verify them by scientific process or historical data. God doesn't need to be proven; only believed. "The just shall live by faith" (Romans 1:17).

In the next chapter I will answer, by the Bible, more objections which are prominently and erroneously taught.

CHAPTER 7

Some Objections and Spiritual Abuses

With increased acceptance of Holy Spirit baptism worldwide, it seems inevitable that erroneous teaching will occur. Unscrupulous people who become enamored of the drama and appeal of the experience are sometimes drawn away from its sacred and noble character. They lose sight of the benefits that God intends for it to bring to the individual and to the church in general. They succumb to the temptation to imitate the genuine experience of the Holy Spirit baptism by fabricating a cheap and carnal facsimile.

Such behavior brings shameful reproach on the valid Pentecostal Movement, which has respect and acceptance in most religious communities of Christianity. For the most part, questionable groups are unorganized, independent bodies whose leaders reject accountability. This is probably because their practices will not stand up under close supervision by a reputable organization. This is not said to discredit all independent churches, however; many are honorable, orthodox and as genuine as any organized church. They are justly given the same respect and acceptance as affiliated bodies.

In view of the many instances of spiritual abuse, excesses and erroneous practices I have encountered in the 48 countries in which I have conducted pastoral seminars, revival crusades and other ministry, I feel compelled to touch briefly upon a practice which seems to occur more often than others. Descendants of Simon the sorcerer in Samaria (see Acts 8) seem to be alive and well in many parts of the world, including America.

The Error of Teaching Believers to Speak in Tongues

This unscriptural practice seems to have had its origin in neo-Pentecostal groups who deplore the phrase, "Tarry ye . . . until ye be endued [baptized] with power from on high [the Holy Spirit]" (Luke 24:49). They proclaim that tarrying is unnecessary. (It should be noted that neo-Pentecostal and psuedo-Pentecostal groups are not representative of the World Pentecostal Fellowship.)

To circumvent the requirement of Jesus to tarry, some have concocted different forms of trickery to *teach* their followers to speak in tongues. This idea is so repulsive it hardly deserves attention, but it should be addressed.

Note how the term *tarry* originated.

- After His resurrection Jesus met with the 11 apostles and others (v. 33).
- He revealed Himself to them and invited them to behold His hands and to touch Him (v. 39).
- He reiterated the Great Commission (v. 47).
- He gave them another promise of the baptism with the Holy Spirit: "And, behold, I send the promise of my Father upon you: but tarry ye in the city of Jerusalem, until ye be endued with power from on high" (v. 49).
- The 11 apostles and those who were with them obeyed the Lord. "They worshipped him, and returned to Jerusalem with great joy: and were continually in the temple, praising and blessing God" (vv. 52, 53).

It is possible and not uncommon to receive the baptism in the Holy Spirit immediately after being converted. This sequence is the ideal. Experience teaches, however, that it does not always happen this way.

Today many seekers find themselves as those to whom Jesus spoke—unaware of the Holy Spirit baptism and/or without knowledge of how to go about seeking to be filled with His power. Not even the apostles knew how to instruct them. But they did know to obey Christ's command! They were "continually in the temple, praising and blessing God" (v. 53). Ten days later, "when the day of Pentecost was fully come" (Acts 2:1), they were with others in the Upper Room and received the baptism in the Holy Spirit (see Acts 2:1-4).

They spoke with "other tongues, as the Spirit gave them utterance" (v. 4). No teaching. No rehearsing. No practicing syllables. The Spirit gave them utterance. As *He* gave the utterance, *they* spoke! Anything less than this is carnal fabrication and a trickery that should be rejected by everyone.

The Holy Spirit does not need our assistance, He only needs our submission, yielding and obedience to Him. The idea of humans controlling or operating the Holy Spirit instead of us being controlled and anointed by Him has absolutely no support in the Bible. From this erroneous teaching has come the practice of learning a *prayer language*. The practice is premised on scriptures that makes no such reference at all.

Those scriptures are Paul's statements in 1 Corinthians 14:15: "I will pray with the spirit, and I will pray with the understanding also"; and Romans 8:26: "Likewise the Spirit also helpeth our infirmities: for we know not what we should pray for as we ought: but the Spirit itself maketh intercession for us with groanings which cannot be uttered."

In the Corinthian statement, Paul was showing the work of the Holy Spirit in lifting up the individual who needs spiritual refreshment. In doing so, the Spirit may motivate the person to pray or sing enthusiastically and joyfully. At His will and discretion the Holy Spirit may begin to give utterances in a tongue unknown to the individual. In praying or singing in an unknown tongue, the individual is edified (1 Corinthians 14:4).

In Romans 8:22, Paul deals with the turmoil of a sin-cursed world that "groaneth and travaileth in pain." Living in such a world, we are confused and frustrated with things we confront. We "know not what we should pray for as we ought" (v. 26), and it is in such times and circumstances that a special benefit of the Holy Spirit baptism comes into focus. The Spirit himself "maketh intercession for us"(v. 26).

Perhaps every Spirit-filled pastor, at some time in his ministry, has been inexplicably awakened at night with an irresistible urge to get up and pray for one of his members. He didn't know why or how to pray, but he began to pray earnestly. Then the Holy Spirit prayed through him in an unknown tongue. He may never know what the burden was all about, but he knows that one of his sheep is loved and cared for by the Holy Spirit.

In both the above scriptures Paul was clearly describing how the "he that searcheth the hearts knoweth what is the mind of the Spirit, because he maketh intercession for the saints according to the will of God (Romans 8:27).

In both cases, Paul speaks of the Holy Spirit's action being a spontaneous and deliberate act. He moves on His own prerogative, needing no action or priming from the individual. In neither case is learning a prayer language stated or implied. The anointing is the same as when one initially speaks in tongues on receiving the Holy Spirit baptism. Any voluntary verbalizing in an unintelligible gibberish is without meaning or substance.

Honest-hearted and sincere Christians have said to me, "When I received the Holy Spirit, someone taught me to speak in tongues. What should I do now?" In the most tender and sincere manner possible, I replied, "I am sorry someone communicated this error to you.

"You don't have to be satisfied with an imitation or gimmick, because God wants you to be baptized in the Holy Spirit; and when you are, He (the Spirit) will speak for Himself without anybody's assistance. I will be glad to pray with you until you receive the Spirit baptism."

The Remedy of Teaching Biblical Truth

How sad it is to see the hurt and disappointment those who have been misled experience over what they have missed when they learn the truth from God's Word. Tarrying for the baptism in the Holy Spirit is not always necessary, but it should never be disparaged or discouraged by anyone.

It doesn't take God a long time to baptize anyone in the Holy Spirit, but it does take some people longer to totally yield to the Spirit or to develop a spiritual hunger for more of God. We just need to be willing to do whatever it takes! The time and the efforts are nothing compared to the benefits. This gift is for you. Other practices are questionable at best, but to itemize all of them may sound petty.

I will repeat Paul's charge to "let all things be done decently and in order" (1 Corinthians 14:40). This should be sufficient to cause us to seek earnestly the will of the Holy Spirit. We must be obedient and yielded to Him, but we must also be careful that no carnal motive is involved in our response to His will.

In 1 Corinthians 12—14, Paul is dealing with spiritual excesses and abuses in the Corinthian church. He gave detailed and candid instructions for correcting three errors:

- the misuse of speaking with tongues,
- the operation of the gifts of the Spirit, and
- the Lord's Supper.

With regret, I confess that in some Pentecostal circles there remain some of these excesses and abuses. They serve as a basis for some critics of Pentecost to oppose and resist the baptism in the Holy Spirit. It should be pointed out, however, that Paul did not suggest that the church refuse to embrace the people receiving the baptism in the Holy Spirit because error had arisen. He gave instructions on how to correct the problem and go on with God's blessing upon His people.

There was error and abuse about the observance of the Lord's Supper in the same Corinthian church, but not one person today suggests we do away with the holy sacrament or its observance.

Common sense dictates that we do not abolish the whole to correct error in the part. That would be like the proverbial cutting off a hand to treat an injured finger.

Therefore, let us adhere to Paul's instruction to properly regulate all aspects of the baptism in the Holy Spirit, so all things will be done in decency and in order.

CHAPTER 8

How To Receive the Baptism in the Holy Spirit

In the preceding chapters I have used the Word of God and logical reasoning to show authoritative and conclusive proof of these facts:

1. The baptism in the Holy Spirit was not relegated to the apostles or the early church. It is for Christians of all ages (Acts 2:39).

2. Baptism in the Holy Spirit occurs subsequent to conversion and salvation.

3. The outward initial evidence of Spirit baptism is speaking with tongues, a fact that is undeniably confirmed in both the Bible and history.

4. This gift (Holy Spirit baptism) is for you here and now.

Those who have never been taught this wonderful truth ask, as did the people on the Day of

Pentecost, "Men and brethren, what shall we do?" (Acts 2:37). To paraphrase the question, *What must we do to receive this marvelous experience?*

In this chapter I will do as I have done in previous chapters; I will answer this question with the Word of God. The Bible is the undeniable authority of all teaching and doctrine. Any church teaching, doctrine or spiritual experience which cannot be verified and confirmed by Scripture should be discarded and forgotten because it will not stand the test of time.

The doctrine and experience of Holy Spirit baptism has endured the test of time, the opposition of unbelievers and the abuse of some adherents. It remains a valid reality. Those who experience daily the blessings and benefits of this glorious experience number in the millions worldwide, and the numbers multiply daily. My sincere prayer is that *you* will be added to that number as a result of reading this book!

The Bible is explicit about what was required of those early disciples who were baptized in the Holy Spirit. A look at the incidents recorded in the Bible provides insight. The continuity of requirements in each incident in the Book of Acts is pointed out in the following outline. One can readily see the consistent pattern.

Jerusalem, on the Day of Pentecost
- *They believed in Jesus* (Acts 2:38)
- *They practiced obedience* (1:12, 14)

- *They had a sense of urgency* (v. 13)
- *They worshiped and praised God* (v. 14)
- *They had unity, a oneness of purpose* (2:1)
- *They did as Jesus commanded* (1:4)
- *They listened to a godly leader* (vv.15-26)
- *They were yielded to the Holy Spirit* (2:4)

SAMARIA

- *They believed in Jesus* (Acts 8:5, 6, 12)
- *They practiced obedience* (v. 12)
- *They practiced praying* (v. 15)
- *They had unity of faith and purpose* (v. 6)
- *They were instructed by godly men* (vv. 14-17)
- *They were yielded to the Holy Spirit* (v. 17)

CAESAREA

- *They believed God* (10: 2)
- *They practiced obedience* (vv. 33, 47, 48)
- *They prayed continually* (vv. 2, 30, 31)
- *They practiced personal discipline* (v. 30)
- *They put forth an effort* (vv. 6, 7)
- *They listened to godly men* (vv. 32, 34-48)
- *They yielded to the Holy Spirit* (v. 46)

DAMASCUS, SAUL OF TARSUS

- *He believed in Jesus* (9:6)
- *He obeyed God* (v. 6)
- *He prayed ontinually* (v. 11)
- *He practiced personal discipline* (v. 9)

- *He put forth an effort—he went into the city to the very house the Lord said* (9:6, 11)
- *He was instructed by a godly man* (v. 17)
- *He yielded to the Holy Spirit* (vv. 17, 18)

Ephesus

- *They believed in Jesus* (19:1, 3)
- *They obeyed and* (v. 5)
- *They were nstructed by a godly man* (v. 4)
- *They yielded to the Holy Spirit (vv. 6, 7)*

A serious study of these five instances reveals a conspicuous pattern of conduct and efforts. This is neither an accident nor a coincidence, because God requires the same devotion and commitment of all people.

There are no shortcuts to God's spiritual blessings for anyone. Just as the baptism in the Holy Spirit is available and designed for all people of every age, the conditions to receive are also.

Because of erroneous teachings and practices by those who would deceive, we must look specifically at some of the requirements. I do not wish to make it to appear difficult to be filled with the Spirit, but God is not so obsessed with quantity that He sacrifices quality. Salvation through Jesus Christ is free, but some things are required in order to receive it.

The immediate requirement in the five incidents mentioned above is that a person must first be a Christian, a disciple of Jesus.

BE A CHRISTIAN

One must repent of his or her sins and accept God's forgiveness before being filled with the Holy Spirit. I contend that it is impossible for anyone anywhere to receive the Holy Spirit baptism without first repenting of all sins and turning from the practice of them. Those still living in sin should not even expect to be filled with the Holy Spirit as long as they are still in sin.

Simon the sorcerer in Damascus made an insincere effort to receive salvation (Acts 8:13). He was baptized in water and followed Philip the evangelist everywhere he went; but Simon's deception was exposed when he offered Peter and John money for the power to baptize people in the Holy Spirit. Peter discerned his wicked heart and exposed him, saying:

> Thy money perish with thee, because thou hast thought that the gift of God may be purchased with money. Thou hast neither part nor lot in this matter: for thy heart is not right in the sight of God (vv. 20, 21).

In the case of Saul in Damascus, we witness the dramatic conversion of this religious zealot who, by his own admission, was a blasphemer and persecutor of Christians whom he had put in jail (see Acts 9:1, 2; Galatians 1:13, 14). But his religiosity was nothing more than zeal for Jewish customs and traditions of the laws of the Old Testament.

On the way to Damascus to jail Christian men and women for their faith, God shined a bright light on him that struck him with blindness as he fell down in the dirt. He heard the voice of Jesus say, "Saul, Saul, why persecutest thou me?" (9:4).

Although Acts 9 does not explicitly describe Paul repenting of his sins and accepting Christ as Savior, I personally believe that he did when "he trembling and astonished said, 'Lord, what wilt thou have me to do?'" He repented of his sins and accepted as Savior the same Jesus whom he had been persecuting and fighting.

Others believe that Paul was converted while fasting and praying for three days in a house on Straight Street in Damascus. Still others believe it happened when Ananias laid hands on him and prayed for him. His conversion could have occurred at any of those times, but the important thing is that evidently he did repent, was forgiven, and became a love slave of Jesus Christ.

In Samaria (Acts 8) there was mass repentance when "the people with one accord gave heed unto those things which Philip spake" (v. 6). In Ephesus and in Jerusalem on the Day of Pentecost, those who received had already been converted and had been disciples of Jesus for varying periods of time. Scriptural evidence in both cases shows that repentance and a changed life had been effected in all of them before they were baptized in the Holy Spirit.

Dr. James P. Bowers contends:

> Within the ongoing process of spiritual renewal, additional fillings are possible and a continuing personal appropriation of Godís grace is necessary. The

believer must ìbe filled with the Spiritî continually, as Paul insisted (Ephesians 5:18). The baptism of the Holy Spirit empowers the believer for this ongoing journey and process of transformation in the Spirit.î

Obey in Righteousness

Walking in the Spirit leads the believer into another dimension of the Spirit-filled life—holiness of heart and life. Remember that the Spirit who fills the believer is the "spirit of holiness" (Romans 1:4). Holiness describes the nature of the Holy Spirit and shapes the character of the Spirit-filled believer.

Paul reproved the immorality of the Corinthians with this question, "Know ye not that your body is the temple of the Holy Ghost, which is in you, which ye have of God, and ye are not your own?" (1 Corinthians 6:19).

I have met some who confessed to having been baptized in the Holy Spirit but who exhibited the works of the flesh. Their habits of life and conduct were unbecoming a Christian. Admittedly, I am not their judge; but displays of uncontrolled or carnal appetites in them caused me to seriously question whether they had any experience with the Holy Spirit.

Pray, and Worship God

Another constant among the recipients of the Holy Spirit in the early church is that they were filled as they worshiped and praised God continually. On the Day of Pentecost, the 120 returned from Mount Olivet where they had watched Jesus go back to heaven. In the Upper Room "these all continued with one accord in prayer and supplication" (Acts 1:14).

In Samaria, the city where thousands were converted in Philip's citywide crusade, Luke wrote of the new converts: "There was great joy in that city" (8:8). Apparently, the constant atmosphere of rejoicing, praising and glorifying God led them to be baptized in the Holy Spirit only days later when Peter and John came from Jerusalem and prayed for them (vv. 15-17).

In Damascus, Paul was confined to a house on Straight Street because he had been stricken with blindness. After Paul spent three days in fasting and prayer (vv. 9, 11), God sent Ananias who laid hands upon Paul and prayed for him—both to be healed and to be baptized in the Holy Spirit. When prayer was made, both happened.

In Caesarea, Cornelius prayed always (10:2, 4). This brought him into such divine favor that God sent an angel from heaven with good news for the centurion. Cornelius's testimony was, "Four days ago I was fasting until this hour; and at the ninth hour I prayed in my house, and, behold, a man stood before me in bright clothing" (v. 30).

When people fast and pray, God listens. Cornelius and many of his relatives and friends were baptized in the Holy Spirit only a few days later.

Regardless of the method or form of worshiping God you prefer to use, the act of worship is what God honors. In the Book of Acts, the prevailing tone of descriptions of those who publicly worshiped God was that of fervency, praise, exuberance, excitement and outward display. However, there were also those who worshiped quietly, reserved and with form. Both can find validation in the Bible.

I have three sons. When they were boys and I gave each of them money, two of them would be excited outwardly with glee and thanks. The other one would quietly say, "Thanks, Dad," and put the money in his pocket. That did not mean that two were more thankful than the one son; it only meant that they were different individuals.

The dominant and most important issue is that we worship God sincerely from our hearts, and worship Him "in spirit and in truth" (John 4:23).

Cultivate a Sense of Urgency

Another element we see in the early disciples is a sense of urgency in their efforts to receive the baptism in the Holy Spirit. Notice particularly the urgency that motivated the 120 on the Day of Pentecost. In Acts, Luke described it in this manner:

> And, being assembled together with them, commanded them that they should not depart from Jerusalem, but wait [tarry, if you please] for the promise of the Father, which, saith he, ye have heard of me(1:4).

In giving this direct and unquestioned mandate to the disciples, Jesus removed all options or alternatives. The Holy Spirit baptism was necessary then and it remains so today! The choice is not ours; Jesus made the choice and commanded it.

Whether you receive the Holy Spirit baptism is not an option with you; if you want to obey God and please Him, you will do whatever it takes to be filled with His wonderful Spirit. The disciples obviously felt that way because "then returned they unto Jerusalem from the mount called Olivet, which is from Jerusalem a sabbath day's journey. And when they were come in, they went up into an upper room" (Acts 1:12, 13).

Immediately after hearing Jesus's command, the disciples obeyed. When they went into the city, they did not go to their homes or their jobs. They went straight to the upper room with singleness of purpose: "These all continued with one accord in prayer and supplication" (v. 14).

We readily see that these seekers were on a mission. They were neither placid nor passive. They had a command to obey and a task to accomplish. They gave themselves to prayer and supplication. The word *supplication* means to "beseech earnestly." It removes any passivity, neutrality or lethargy in our attitude toward our quest for God's promise.

They went to the Upper Room daily for to pray, praise and worship God. They received the Holy Spirit baptism 10 days later. They were obviously so lost in their efforts and so consumed by their pursuit that they were oblivious to the onlookers who crowded the Upper Room. So "when this was noised abroad, the multitude came together, and were confounded, because that every man heard them speak in his own language" (2:6).

Caught up in the ecstasy of praise and worship to God, they neither heard nor were disturbed by the behavior of the crowd. "[The onlookers] were all amazed, and were in doubt, saying one to another, What meaneth this? Others mocking said, These men are full of new wine" (Acts 2:12, 13).

Today, seekers of the Holy Spirit must be prepared to deal with the fact that there will be hindrances to seeking the blessing. Not everyone will understand or agree with your purpose or efforts. You must not be dismayed or distracted, but must continue relentlessly in your obedience to Christ's command and the pursuit of the gift He has promised you. The reward will be the glorious, exciting experience of being baptized in the Holy Spirit!

Remember that none of the people who were onlookers, doubters, critics, or slanderers in the Upper Room received the baptism in the Holy Spirit. Only the 120 who were devoted to worshiping, praising and obeying God received this precious gift of promise.

Awareness of this fact brings us to another vitally important requirement contained in the five instances in Acts where people received the Holy Spirit baptism.

LISTEN TO GODLY INSTRUCTION

In each case cited in this chapter, those who received the baptism in the Holy Spirit were instructed by a godly person who gave them nurturing counsel and prayer.

- At Pentecost, Simon Peter gave the leadership even though he was a seeker and a recipient of the gift just as were the others in the room.
- In Samaria, Peter and John gave instructions and laid hands on the seekers. As the apostles prayed for them, they were baptized in the Holy Spirit.
- In Damascus, Ananias, a layman, prayed for and instructed Saul.
- In Caesarea, the apostle Peter again gave instruction and prayer to Cornelius and his family and friends who were filled with the Holy Spirit.
- In Ephesus, Paul gave instructions and prayer for the 12 disciples who were baptized in the Holy Spirit.

The constant pattern in these instances was not coincidental. Godly instruction is too important to be left to chance. It is important for seekers to put themselves in an environment that is conducive to receiving the Holy Spirit.

You will not receive encouragement or instructions to seek the baptism in the Holy Spirit from every church in your city. In fact, some will even forbid you to do so. Therefore, it is unlikely that you will receive the gift of the Holy Spirit in a setting where the experience is opposed, taught against or discouraged.

Understand me clearly. I do not take this position in an attempt to proselyte members from any church. But would you go to a Jewish synagogue, Moslem mosque or Buddhist temple to learn about Jesus and how to become a Christian? I think not.

Nor will you find help or instruction on how to receive the baptism in the Holy Spirit in a church where the gift is not experienced or taught by the leaders of the church.

The Bible did not make an oversight or use fill-in words to describe the unity and singleness of purpose that characterized the early seekers of the Holy Spirit baptism.

- "These all continued with one accord" (Acts 1:14).
- "And when the day of Pentecost was fully come, they were all with one accord" (2:1).
- "And the people with one accord gave heed unto those things which Philip spake" (8:6).
- "And Cornelius waited for them, and had called together his kinsmen and near friends" (10:24).

How difficult it is for anyone to find God's perfect will in the presence of disunity, doubt, opposition or resistance to His word and will. There is probably a fundamental Pentecostal church near your home whose pastor and members have experienced this great and marvelous experience I have described. They will love you, receive you, and pray for you to receive God's promised gift.

I urge you to seek them out, attend their services and be filled with the Holy Spirit.

This gift is for you—now!

To the Pastor

My dear colleague, I pray God that your members may never be able to say what the 12 Ephesian disciples told Paul, "We have not so much as heard whether there be any Holy Ghost" (Acts 19:2). I shudder for any pastor who lives under an indictment of those words spoken by his members. What defense can we plead in the Day of Judgment?

In my 52 years of ministry I have always had a special time of prayer and help for seekers of Holy Spirit baptism. Every pastor should enthusiastically teach his people the vital truth of God's Word regarding the baptism in the Holy Spirit. Encourage them, instruct them, lay hands on them and pray for them until they are baptized in the Holy Spirit. Plan a service for seekers and saturate it with much prayer and study.

The doctrinal position on this subject by your denomination is not nearly as important or as imposing to you as the awesome responsibility God has given you when He placed you as the shepherd of the flock—His people. I challenge you, my brother and sister, to examine the scriptures in this book with an open mind and a sincere desire to know God's truth for your ministry.

This gift is for *you* and all your members. Obey God regardless of the consequences! There can be only blessings and spiritual profit by doing so.

An Appeal to the Honest Seeker

My brother or sister, in these few pages you have adequate evidence from God's Word to show that this gift of the baptism in the Holy Spirit is for you. As I have written each word I have felt the anointing of the Holy Spirit. I honestly feel He has inspired and approved what is contained in this book.

You can disagree with me, but can you argue with God's Word? I have written these pages with fear and trembling, and I pray that you will read them with the same sincerity.

Why not embark on a quest for a new dimension of life in the Spirit today?

- Experience a closer relationship with God than you have ever had before.

- Realize a greater anointing of God's power in your life or ministry than you have ever witnessed.

- Cultivate a more intense desire to live a holy life and turn away from worldly activity and carnal desires.

- Attend a church where the baptism in the Holy Spirit is experienced and taught.

- Seek the Holy Spirit baptism every opportunity you have, and don't be discouraged if you do not receive Him at the first effort.

You benefit every time you pray and seek God. It does not take God a long time to fill you with

His Spirit, but it may take you much praying to develop the right relationship to Jesus in order to receive the baptism in the Holy Spirit.

Remember, do not seek tongues, but seek rather the fullness of His grace and power. Tongues will come by the will of the Holy Spirit when He fills your soul with His presence. When you are baptized in the Holy Spirit, you will speak in tongues. As you praise God and worship Him gladly, the Holy Spirit will give utterance (inspiration) and you will speak (Acts 2:4).

Be careful from whom you receive counsel and instruction—especially on how to receive the baptism in the Holy Spirit. Jesus' command to you is to receive Holy Spirit baptism. It is His delight and pleasure to fill you with His great power and presence. You don't have to beg Him to do it; just remember God's Word: "This promise [gift] is unto you" (2:39).

After you have read and studied this book, I would be delighted to hear the testimony of your experience. Whether it is positive or negative, I would like to know about it. You may write me to share your testimony.

Dr. B. G. Hamon
5000 Jesse Aycock Circle
Garfield, Georgia 30425
U.S.A.

BIBLIOGRAPHY

Bowers, James P. "Experiencing the Baptism in the Holy Spirit." *Endued with Power.* Cleveland, TN: Pathway Press, 1995.

Bruce, F.F. *Commentary on the Book of Acts.* Grand Rapids: Erdmans, 1954.

Brumbach, Carl. *What Meaneth This?* Springfield, MO: Gospel Publishing House, 1947.

Calvin, John. *Commentary Upon the Acts of the Apostles.* Grand Rapids: Erdmans, 1949.

Carroll, R. Leonard. "Glossolalia: From Pentecost to the Reformation." *The Glossolalia Phenomenon.* Ed. Wade H. Horton. Cleveland, TN: Pathway Press, 1966, 65-94.

Conn, Charles W. "Glossolalia and the Scriptures." *The Glossolalia Phenomenon.* Ed. Wade H. Horton. Cleveland, TN: Pathway Press, 1966, 21-65.

Conn, Charles W. *Why Men Go Back.* Cleveland, Tennessee: Pathway Press, 1966.

Cutten, William B. *Twentieth Century Encyclopaedia of Religious Knowledge.* Ed. Lefferts A. Loetcher. Grand Rapids: Baker Book House, 1955, 1118.

Gause, R.H. "The Holy Spirit's Relation to the Believer." *Church of God Evangel,* Volume 47, Number 40. December 10, 1956, 7-11.

Gee, Donald. "Pentecost, a Word with Many Meanings." *Pentecostal Evangel,* Number 2654, March 21, 1965, 6, 7.

Hargrave, Vessie D. "Glossolalia: Reformation to the Twentieth Century." *The Glossolalia Phenomenon.* Ed. Wade H. Horton. Cleveland, TN: Pathway Press, 1966, 97-139.

Henry, Matthew (1935). *Commentary on the Whole Bible.* New York: Fleming H. Revell Co., 1935.

Hughes, Ray H. *What Is Pentecost?* Cleveland, TN: Pathway Press, 1963.

Hughes, Ray H. "The Baptism in the Holy Ghost." *Church of God Evangel*, Volume 55, Number 14, May 31, 1965, 18-22.

McDonald, William G. "Glossolalia in Acts Analyzed." *On Guard*, Volume 9, Number 10, October 1969, 8-10.

Olson, Arnold T. *This We Believe*. Minneapolis: Free Church Publications, 1961.

Paulk, Sr., Earl P. *The Pentecostal Baptism*. Cleveland, TN: Church of God Evangelism and Home Missions Department, n.d.

Pearlman, Myer. *Knowing the Doctrines of the Bible.* Springfield, MO: Gospel Publishing House, 1937.

Robertson, A.T. *Word Pictures in the New Testament*. New York: Harper & Row, 1930.

Schaff, Phillip. *History of the Apostolic Church.* Springfield, MO: Gospel Publishing House, 1936.

"Speaking in Tongues." *Catholic Biblical Encyclopaedia.* Eds. John E. Mueller and Kathryn Sullivan, 1956.

"Speaking in Tongues." *Time,* August 15, 1960, 55.

"Tongues, gift of." *Encyclopedia Brittanica,* Vol. XXII, 1958 ed.

Trapp, John. *Commentary on the New Testament.* (rev. ed.). Grand Rapids: Zondervan, 1958.

Triplett, Bennie S. *A Contemporary Study of the Holy Spirit.* Cleveland, TN: Pathway Press, 1970.

Wesley, John. *One Volume New Testament Commentary.* Grand Rapids: Baker Book House, 1958.